AF663112

Communities as Vote Banks

Elections in India

Communities as Vote Banks
Elections in India

Edited By

Zaheer Ali

AAKAR

Communities as Vote Banks: Elections in India
Edited by Zaheer Ali

© Editor

First Published 2020
Reprinted 2022

ISBN 978-93-5002-659-5

All rights reserved. No part of this book may be reproduced or transmitted, in any form or by any means, without the prior permission of the Publisher.

Published by
AAKAR BOOKS
28 E Pocket IV, Mayur Vihar Phase I
Delhi 110 091 India
aakarbooks@gmail.com

Laser Typeset at
Sakshi Computers, Delhi

Printed at
Sapra Brothers, Noida.

Contents

Caste

Region

Media

Reforms

Foreword

Replicating its unfathomable geographical diversity, India is a unique amalgamation of infinite cultures, ethnicities, languages, religions, cuisines, art and the list goes on. In particular, India hosts over two thousand ethnicities, more than 19,500 languages/dialects[1] spoken as mother tongues (including 22 languages recognised in the Eighth Schedule of the Constitution) and is blessed with six main official religions–Hinduism, Islam, Christianity, Sikhism, Jainism and Buddhism–while 79.38 lakh people practise "other religions". Our country's canvas of land is decorated with such vibrant colours of diversity. To respect this vast reality, our constitutional forefathers defined India as a secular democratic republic.

A democracy–which in simple terms is, "of the people, for the people and by the people"–for India was to be a temporary and disastrous experiment owing to its diversity as per international observers. Ramachandra Guha in his book, *India After Gandhi: The History of the World's Largest Democracy*, quoted Sir John Strachey saying in 1880, "is the first and most essential thing to learn about India–that there is not, and never was an India, or even any country of India possessing, according to any European ideas, any sort of unity, physical, political, social or religious". He further underlined

1. https://indianexpress.com/article/india/more-than-19500-mother-tongues-spoken-in-india-census-5241056/

the national sympathies "should ever extend to India generally, that men of the Punjab, Bengal, the Northwestern Provinces, and Madras, should ever feel that they belong to one Indian nation, is impossible".

Celebrating its 70th anniversary of being a constitutional democracy, India has proved everyone wrong with its inherent mutual harmony, the much celebrated unity in diversity. The central reason for the closely-knit nature of our society is the safeguards in the Constitution of India. Be it the fundamental rights to practise religion (Articles 25-28), to preserve culture, language or script (Articles 29-30), prohibition of discrimination based on religion, race or caste (Article 15) or Schedule 5 and 6 protecting rights and interests of the tribal areas or federal set up of the Indian polity acknowledging the regional diversity, the law of the land roused the faith of different communities in the nation and its policies. Being an electoral democracy, the architects of our Constitution ensured political equality as well by extending the right to vote and contest to all sections of Indian society. As a result, the political parties mirror the social composition of the country making every constituent community a crucial vote bank. However, the reality has not been reflected in the Lok Sabha. According to the Association for Democratic Reforms, the 17th Lok Sabha has 90.4 per cent Hindus and just 5.2 per cent Muslims, which is starkly different from their real composition of 79.8 per cent and 14.2 per cent of the population respectively. While the regional diversity has been maintained due to the freeze in delimitation, the more worrisome has been the gender composition wherein women comprise only 14.6 per cent of the total 545 seats in the Lok Sabha–nowhere close to their 48.5 per cent population in India. The situation would have been worse had it not been for the reservation of seats in the Parliament for SC and ST communities: other than the 84 and 47 seats reserved for the respective communities, the 17th Lok Sabha has two seats won by an SC candidate and five seats won by an ST candidate. The lower house remains largely dominated by the upper caste with 232 seats on its side, while the OBC is a distant second with 120 seats.

The imbalanced representation in the Parliament manifests a larger problem at the root level: social inequality. Dr. B.R. Ambedkar in his speech at the Constituent Assembly rightly stated, "Political democracy cannot last unless there lies at the base of it social democracy". He adds, "...If we continue to deny it (social and economic equality) for long, we will do so only by putting our political democracy in peril. We must remove this contradiction at the earliest possible moment or else those who suffer from inequality will blow up the structure of political democracy which this Assembly has laboriously built". If past instances are anything to go by, India's social democracy has been in peril, and its effect on political democracy has been largely reported on by every international democracy observer. India has been on a consistent decline in the category of "Social Group Equality" and "Freedom of Religion" in the Global State of Democracy Index. Under the Varieties of Democracy Index, India is on a steep decline in the "Egalitarian Democracy" Index, while the country has been on the lowest rank since 2006 in the EIU's Democracy Index and is categorised as a "flawed democracy".

Against this backdrop, it becomes increasingly important to analyse how affected communities vote in what is described as the largest festival of a democracy. It is imperative to understand how such communities respond to the varied electoral campaigns of the political parties and whether their representation in Parliament is in the list of their electoral demands. This book perfectly captures the voting behaviour of sections defined on the lines of religion, caste, region and ethnicity. It zeroes in on whether the inter-community cohesiveness is replicated in their demands and electoral choices or they continue to remain mutually exclusive.

The book does not stop at comparative politics within communities but also explores various electoral reforms, which could uplift India from the tag of flawed democracy to the greatest. One of them discussed is the electoral system of proportional representation. This system could prove to be a shot in the arm for representation of regional and community specific political parties. There have been several instances wherein high vote share failed to result in seats. For instance, the Bahujan Samaj Party earned 20 per cent and 4 per cent vote share at state and national level respectively (third largest amongst parties, in both), but could not score a seat in the 2014 Lok Sabha elections. In contrast the Trinamool National Congress and All India Anna Draveda Munnetra Kazhagam won 34 and 37 seats respectively with vote share at 3.8 and 3.3 per cent respectively. The chapter is a compilation of many such instances with elaboration on various electoral systems in place across the world. It aims to belie the negative aspects of First Past the Post system in favour of a better inclusive legislature.

Finally, I strongly recommend this book to every election enthusiast who wants to analyse the voting patterns of every vote bank and make sense of the puzzle that Indian politics is. It will shed some light on all the myths that we have been told since our childhood on how a section votes and carries with itself an ability to lead the movement on bringing the communities, reduced into mere vote banks, in the electoral map of political parties and the policy makers.

There may be certain views and opinions of the writers with which I may differ, but I would wholeheartedly defend their right to hold those views.

May 2020 **S.Y. Quraishi**

Former Chief Election Commissioner of India

Preface

It is arguable that electoral studies serve any useful purpose. The critics point out that most pre-poll or exit-poll predictions, more often than not, prove to be incorrect and, therefore, such activities are futile exercises with self-chosen designation of academic studies. Psephology, as a result, for the critics is a highly ostentatious branch of the science of politics that should be dispensed with. Others point out that whether the predictions are on the mark or off the mark that makes absolutely no difference to the fortunes of contesting political parties or to the people at large. These are extreme views that are obviously beyond the academic discourse. Having said this, it must be spelled out that this volume is not a pre-poll or post-poll study of any particular election. It comprises the papers presented by the leading social scientists of India on the voting behaviour of various communities.

The community formation in India takes place on account of various agents–religion, caste, region, language and so on. This volume encompasses studies of electoral behaviour of the communities formed on the bases of religion, caste and region. Additionally there is a paper dealing with the role of media in the overall process of electioneering. There are also two papers recommending significant reforms in the Indian electoral system. One suggests reforms are required to ensure proper weightage to be given to the political parties in terms of seats in the legislature commensurate with their share in the votes polled. The other paper emphasizes the need to use the latest technological devices for conducting elections to increase the involvement of the electorates.

Though India is the largest democracy of the contemporary world, it is not without its flaws. In the global Democracy Index it has always occupied a rank that hardly makes Indians proud. In the recent years, however, it has drastically slipped much lower. According to the Economist Group though almost half the countries of the world declare themselves to be democracies, the number of 'real' democracies is less than 20. It was 19 in 2017 when India was ranked 32. A year later it slipped to 42nd place among 165 countries that have some features of democracy. Interestingly, the Economist Group does not enlist the US among 'full democracies'; it is also in the company of 'flawed democracies.

There may be arguments and counter-arguments about the parameters that are given weightage by democracy watchers such as the Economist Group but the fact remains that in India it is not simply the political membership, i.e. citizenship of an individual that is adequate enough to be of some value in electioneering. It is the religion, caste, region and so on that make an individual a part of some collective that counts. This volume critiques the crucial role the communities play in elections in India while also making attempts to find out why they do so.

Vasai **Zaheer Ali**

Acknowledgements

I, on behalf of Centre for Promotion of Democracy and Secularism (CPDS), would like, first of all, to express a deep sense of gratitude to Dr. Balaji N. Kendre, Director of University of Mumbai's Rajiv Gandhi Centre for Contemporary Studies, who played a proactive role in organising a national conference on 'Communities as Vote Banks: Electoral Behaviour of Indian Voters.' It must be underscored that without Dr. Kendre's wholehearted support the conference would not have been as fruitful as it was. I must also state that Dr. Murlidhar Kurhade, Dean, Humanities, University of Mumbai, despite having a tight schedule was kind enough to spare half a day to inaugurate the conference and deliver the inaugural address. I sincerely appreciate the academic commitment of my friend Dr. Karli Srinivasulu, Senior Fellow, ICSSR and formerly Professor & Head, Department of Political Science, Osmania University, Hyderabad for delivering an insightful Keynote Address of the event. Thanks are also due to Dr. Jose George, formerly Professor and Head, Department of Civics and Politics, University of Mumbai for consenting to be the Chief Guest of the valedictory session and deliver the valedictory address. Besides, he also presented a paper that is part of this volume. I must express gratitude to my mentor-friend, Ibrahim Rungla, who despite his advanced age took the trouble to be present in the inaugural session of the conference.

With a heavy heart, I remember the spirited contribution of Dr. Afaq Khan in the capacity of Secretary, Centre for Promotion of Democracy and Secularism to the Centre and also to organising the conference. Sadly, he died soon after the conclusion of the conference. His dedication to academics and his social activism will always be cherished by the members of the CPDS.

I must express my appreciation to Dr. Gautam Gawali and Dr. Mohammad Fayyaz who chaired the two core sessions of the conference. Besides the academics whose papers appear in this volume, the other scholars such as Dr. S.N. Sahu, Dr. Mrudul Nile, Dr. N. Venkatesu E., G. Srinivasa Rao and Prof. Neetin Sonawane deserve my thanks for their intellectual contributions. I, in particular, thank Prof. Neetin Sonawane who helped in various ways to make the conference a memorable event.

Among friends I express my gratitude to Mohammad Wajihuddin of the *Times of India*, Flory D'Souza and Sibtain Naqvi who continue to render yeoman service to CPDS in its academic ventures.

Z. A.

Introduction

Zaheer Ali

India is a plural society in the true sense of the term. Its heterogeneity is unique because no other country in the world can claim to have such diversity in terms of religion, caste, language, region, ethnicity, race and culture. Additionally, economic standing too divides people into classes. Poverty is an all-pervading concern all over the world. However, stark poverty affecting huge sections of masses is typical of India. Despite visible development in various fields, mass poverty is a ubiquitous phenomenon cutting across religious boundaries and caste limits. Nevertheless, poverty is much more in evidence among the marginalised sections of Indian society, for instance, Muslims and Dalits. At this point the intention is not to critique the causes of poverty in India; the focal point right now is to underscore the fact that poverty of the electorates does affect their voting behaviour.

The adherents of all major religions of the world–Hinduism, Islam, Christianity, Buddhism, Jainism, Judaism and Zoroastrianism live here. Though it is a matter of pride that followers of almost all the religions live in amity and harmony in a country which is predominantly Hindu, it must also be taken into account that religious diversity occasionally get in the way of judicious functioning of democratic governance. The minorities are neither legally discriminated against nor do they face impediments in the practice of their respective faiths. Even so, they in quite a few matters face social discrimination because legal equality does not necessarily ensure social equality. The Indian Constitution is one of the finest statutes of the world that is committed to establish a democratic, socialist, secular republic with a pledge to make available justice, liberty and equality to all its citizens. Indian society, however, is not absolutely liberal or egalitarian. The political parties that hold power have to struggle between upholding the law and satisfying the demands and aspirations of their vote banks. Seeking votes in the name of religion is a corrupt practice as per Section 123 (3) of the Representation of People's Act. This section has been further fortified in 2017 by a seven-judge constitution bench of the Supreme Court which delivered that seeking votes in the name of religion, caste and community amounted to corrupt practice and for that reason election of a candidate could be set aside. In order to get around the law during the course of elections quite a few political parties find ways and means to woo the targeted religious communities to get their votes. Religion, therefore, plays a pivotal role in Indian elections.

What makes Indian society unique is the caste system. Caste is a hierarchical social institution which, in many ways, more momentous than even religion. Historically speaking, though caste had been a manufactured characteristic, over the centuries it has acquired the status of a primordial institution; one can change his religion but he cannot get rid of caste affiliation. According to the verdict mentioned above of the Supreme Court, seeking votes invoking caste affiliation is also a corrupt electoral practice. Nonetheless, the role of caste in Indian elections is too pronounced. Caste plays a key role in almost every aspect of electioneering. A few political parties are exclusively created and promoted for the protection of the interests of certain caste groups. It goes without saying that these political parties have devised methods to skirt the aforementioned legal restriction. Though it is true that at the national level political processes including elections, the role of caste seems to remain quiescent, caste plays a prominent role at state-level and village-level elections. One can find the role of caste in the distribution of tickets by all the major political parties, in their approach to highlight the public issues, formation of councils of ministers and also in the selection of officers of the legislatures. Except for extraordinary circumstances, the Indian voters usually vote in line with their caste affiliations. It explains why numerically dominant castes (*bahujan samaj*) in different states also dominate the state political scenario.

Then there is language. Though the Constitution of India recognises 22 languages, there are minimum 800 languages and more than 2000 dialects that are spoken across India. The very fact that reorganisation of states in India has been done on a linguistic basis, language has naturally acquired significance to influence the electoral process. In a broader sense there exists a tacit rivalry between the Centre's official language, Hindi, and various regional languages, in particular, of South India. In the past this rivalry had led to violent protests and ugly riots particularly after 1965 when the Centre, in accordance with the constitutional stipulation had made attempts to do away with English as one of the two official languages. The people in Southern India saw in the move a conspiracy of the North Indian politicians to colonise the South and emasculate the languages, cultures, traditions and values derived from Dravidian origin. The riots in the South, in particular, in Tamil Nadu, were so horrific that the Centre had to shelve its policy of discontinuation of English as one of the two official languages almost indefinitely. Besides this, there have been instances of political trouble on the issue of language. The Hindi-Punjabi conflict led to bifurcation of the state into Punjab and Haryana. The inception of a political party, Shiv Sena, was actually for establishing the supremacy of Marathi and people in the Mumbai metropolitan region. Mumbai which is the capital of Maharashtra is a cosmopolitan city in the true sense where people of all faiths, regions and linguistic groups reside. Though the people of Marathi origin constitute the largest linguistic group, it is about one-fifths of the total population of the metropolis. With a view to assert the dominance of Maharashtrians in the metropolis, the Shiv Sena was formed which adopted a militant approach to implement its policies. Presently, Shiv Sena is one of the significant regional parties of India. Recently, the creation of Telangana out of a larger Telugu state of Andhra Pradesh cannot be exclusively explained on the basis of linguism. It was the outcome of uneven development of sub-regions of the state. It must, therefore, be underscored that linguism and regionalism are closely interconnected.

Regional diversity is a complex phenomenon because in addition to geographical diversity it is enmeshed in linguistic, cultural and also racial factors. Regionalism in India is an important factor that induces the electorates to vote for the protection of the interests of their respective regions. It is an accepted democratic behaviour because regionalism in India does not have a dimension of secessionism though immediately after independence, the Dravidian leaders in the erstwhile state of Madras had mulled over creating a separate sovereign state of Dravidistan. Nonetheless, since the enforcement of the Indian Constitution, secessionist tendencies have been cast off from the politics of South India. In the states of the North-East, particularly in Nagaland, secessionism has been a dominant agenda. In the current scenario the region seems to have reconciled with the stark political realities by opting to resolve various problems of the region by affirming their faith in the Constitution of India.

Although racial multiplicity is often pushed under the carpet by the leading political actors, its presence and impact over political processes can hardly be undermined. The racial issue lurks in the political aspirations of the people of the South and of the North-East. The leaders in these regions have always been circumspect to any policy or programme of the Centre that might be remotely linked to the dominance of the North Indian people who are purportedly of Aryan stock. Regional and racial factors result in the cultural diversity which is conspicuous by the presence of varied cuisines, festivals, attires and customs. In a sense Indian pluralism must be commended because it creates a multi-coloured and kaleidoscopic social order that apportion a vim and vigour to the life of the people. In purely sociological terms it sounds credible but politically it might pose serious problems if left unchecked.

India, in addition to the most pluralistic society, is also the largest democracy of the world. Conducting a nationwide election for the Parliament at least once in five years is a colossal task. India is also a federation having 29 States and 7 Union Territories. The State Legislators, with the exception of Jammu and Kashmir, are also normally elected for a tenure of five years. Consequently, political parties pull out all the stops to capture political power. There are about a dozen political parties that claim the status of national parties (though the Election Commission confers that honour only to seven parties), however, there are many more regional parties confined to a particular state or region. There are many more political parties that are not recognised by the Election Commission. Legally speaking, the number of political parties cannot be restricted and for that reason numbers of political parties have swelled during the last seventy years. In a competitive political democracy, political parties are likely to resort to all kinds of strategies to win elections. For that reason, the divisive factors come in handy to the politicians, an overwhelming majority of whom is far from being scrupulous. In this competitive electoral process, political ideology plays a negligible role. Political parties, as a rule, appeal to the electorates on emotional issues to get hold of their votes. Consequently, the socially divisive factors such as caste, religion, language, and ethnicity are exploited to the hilt by the contesting candidates. It also explains why the divide between rich and poor hardly matters in electoral politics in India. It is the community not the class that is significant in elections in India. Accordingly, different communities have turned into vote banks for different political parties. It may be the antithesis of a true liberal democracy but it is the truth of Indian democracy.

The parliamentary elections of 2019 are being viewed as the most significant from the point of view of supremacy of the Constitution and revival of the idea of a secular democracy. It goes without saying that the major political parties will keep appealing to their respective vote banks to capture political power at the Centre. Nonetheless, it will be interesting to witness whether the customary vote banks continue to vote the way they have been traditionally voting or they show concern to protect the values enshrined in the Constitution of India. In order to have a deeper understanding of the Indian electoral process, the Centre for Promotion of Democracy and Secularism in collaboration with Mumbai University's Rajiv Gandhi Centre for Contemporary Studies had jointly organised a two-day national conference in the last week of January 2019. Scholars from all over India deeply analysed and reflected upon various dimensions of electioneering in the largest democracy of the world. In this volume a selection of the papers that were presented in the conference have been brought together.

The theme of the conference could not be explained in a more thorough and discerning manner by any other contemporary scholar than Dr. K. Srinivasulu, who has been engaged in the study of Indian political processes including the voting behaviour of varied segments of society for long. He underscores the point that the Indian 'political mosaic' is an extremely complex phenomenon considering the heterogeneity of incompatible ideological conflicts. For instance, he points out that the Constitution of India speaks a liberal language with the guarantees of various rights and affirms faith in equality and justice as the cherished values but at the same time there are quite powerful political actors that are committed to *Hindutva*, that, briefly speaking, is the negation of almost all the values enshrined in the basic law of the land. In his view the 'political universe' of the subaltern castes is a home-grown realm mainly inhabited by the exploited sections of India.

While dealing with the concept of community, Srinivasulu brings into focus its innate aspects such as identity, solidarity and the 'possibility of collective decision and action'. He maintains that the idea of vote-bank in India is constructed on patron-client rapport and further he adds that vote-banks are 'forged on caste, religious, sub-regional and linguistic identities'. He observes that the subaltern castes in the contemporary political scenario tend to stand up for their identity and autonomy which makes the leaders of major political parties circumspect while dealing with these castes. In his opinion as caste can be a 'potential unifier', at the same time it can also create 'division and conflict' in society. It is for this reason the dominant castes can easily make use of caste to divide people and realise electoral gains. The political subordination of the lower castes to the dominant castes, Srinivasulu argues, is the root cause of turning the politically weaker castes into vote-banks. Consequently, the lower castes fail to emerge as self-directed political actors to participate on equal terms in the process of governance.

My paper is mainly about Muslim electoral behaviour right from the first General Election in 1952 to the last Parliamentary election of 2014. Additionally, I have also demolished certain myths about the Muslim voting pattern that have been, on purpose, designed and proliferated mostly by the Hindu Right. My first contention is that the Indian Muslims are as heterogeneous a community as the Hindu community. This falsehood that the Muslims constitute a homogeneous social category is mostly spread by the mullahs who prefer to ignore differences among Indian Muslims on account of caste, language, region, ethnicity and race that make them as much a fragmented community as that of Hindus. Muslims' electoral behaviour obviously varies from caste to caste, region to region and so on. The popular perception that the Muslims vote *en masse* is another canard floated by the Hindu communal forces. The noticeable difference between Muslim and Hindu electorates is that most Muslims give precedence to physical security of the community and for that reason they are unlikely to vote for certain political parties belonging to the Hindu Right as they are perceived to be anti-Muslims. This, by and large, can be called a constant feature of most of the Muslim electorates.

It is also important to note that the Muslim voting behaviour has undergone changes during the seventy-year history of Indian democracy. Focusing only on Parliamentary elections the changing pattern may be classified into three major phases. In the first phase spread over from 1951 to 1977, Muslims were for the most part concerned about their security and, therefore, most of them voted for the Congress. In the second phase of twelve years, i.e. from 1977 to 1989, the weakening of the Congress Party had also weakened the dependence of the Muslims on it. They gradually grew disenchanted with the grand old party and showed signs of political self-assurance in their electoral behaviour. In the third phase spanned from 1989 to the present, the most striking incident was the demolition of the Babri Masjid in December 1992, when the Congress was in power at the Centre and the Prime Minister, Narasimha Rao had given assurances of prevalence of law and order. This calamitous incident alienated most Muslims, in particular, in North India from the Congress. In the changed circumstances, the Muslims adopted the method of *strategic voting* which has a two-pronged purposefulness; shun the Congress and at the same time ensure that the Hindu communal forces represented by the BJP do not capture power. This method has had mixed results. It helped certain regional political parties to come to power in their respective states but it could not stop BJP emerging as the strongest political party in the 2014 elections.

In the last section of my paper I make an attempt to demolish some of the myths that are usually associated with the Muslims in India. The first myth is about Muslims voting *en masse.* This myth has sprouted because of the homogeneous image of the community. The reality is that the Muslims are divided on caste, language, region, ethnicity, etc. just like Hindus. The presence of caste groups such as Ashraf, Ajlaf and Arzal make it difficult for all Muslims to vote similarly.

The second myth that the Muslims vote only for Muslim candidates or to the parties that are established exclusively for the Muslims, is ludicrous to say the least. How many Muslims contest the Parliamentary elections and how many of them actually get elected? Like all Hindus do not vote for the political parties that are purportedly established for protecting the interests of the Hindus, all Muslims too do not vote for the so-called Muslim parties. In the context I have argued by showing the dismal political performance of the parties like the Indian Union Muslim League, Majlis-e-

Ittehadul Muslimeen, All India United Democratic Front and the Peace Party. They are confined to a few pockets and could never enjoy the majority support of the Muslims.

The third myth is that the Muslims vote all together for the Congress. This was true mostly in the North till the 1971 Parliamentary elections. It is true that most non-Muslim voters in the Hindi heartland deserted the Congress in 1967 but the Muslims even in that election supported the Congress. Nonetheless, in 1977, the elections held after the Emergency the majority of Muslims, like their countrymen, voted for the Janata Party. Thereafter, in the 1981 and 1984 Lok Sabha elections the voting behaviour of the Muslims was not different from most Indians. It was in 1989, when Rajiv Gandhi launched his election campaign from Ayodhya with a distinct purpose to entice the Hindu voters, the Muslims particularly in North India moved away from the Congress. So the unconditionally and constant Muslim support to the Congress is nothing but a myth. According to an estimate, the Muslim community's overall support for the Congress never exceeded 40 per cent of the electorates casting votes which means 60 per cent of the Muslims have been voting against the Congress.

Similarly the Muslim clerics controlling Muslim voting behaviour is completely false. Though the mullahs accept money from various political parties with the promise to influence voting behaviour of the community, most Muslims, however, ignore their exhortations. Another untruth widely circulated is about the high percentage of Muslims voting. There is no data to prove this canard usually spread by the Hindu Right.

Another paper analysing the electoral behaviour of the Muslims is that of Shuja Shakir. He insists that socio-economic standing and occupational pattern mainly decide the voting behaviour of the Muslims. In this respect their electoral behaviour is like any other religious community. In support of his argument he quotes from a CSDS-Lokniti report about UP Assembly elections of 2012 that says that 'while 26 per cent low-caste Muslims voted for BSP, only 11 per cent of their votes went to Congress'. He cites the figures of other elections too underpinning his contention that since the

Muslim community is a heterogeneous one its voting behaviour is also divergent.

He affirms that though Muslims have not been voting for the BJP, it should not be believed that they are doing it as a calculated strategy to keep the Hindu Right away from power. In his opinion the Muslim voting behaviour is similar to the electoral behaviour of other communities as the Muslim community's "vote choice is driven by performance, party preferences, candidates, welfare policies and leadership among many other things." Citing the data of the 2012 UP Assembly elections again he asserts that there is no difference between the Muslims and others with regard to political participation and proactiveness. By way of conclusion, he cites the observation from a study jointly done by Rahul Verma and Pranav Gupta that "while the presence of the BJP remains an important factor when Muslims make their decision about whom to vote for, that is not their sole parameter. Their choice is as much affected by issues of price rise, corruption, and employment as for any other voter."

The third significant study about the voting behaviour of a religious community is that of Ranu Jain who has perceptively probed the social standing of the Jain community in India and its voting behaviour. Agreeing with Blair's view she avers that historical experience and the socio-political status of a community are momentous factors in determining its voting pattern. She makes a distinction between a minority by force and a minority by will. The Muslims belong to the former category while the Jains fall in the latter. The difference between the two minorities varies in their electoral behaviour. She argues that Jainism as a faith campaigns for individualism while consenting to diversity. Additionally the community is endowed with economic and cultural capital which makes it confident and assertive. Nevertheless she points out the difference between political choices of the Digambar Jains of Karnataka and Maharashtra and the Svetambar Jains of Gujarat and Rajasthan.

Jain philosophical strands such as individualism, relativity and non-absolutism, according to her, help the community to be accepted as a 'non-threatening' segment of the larger society. Jains usually follow the local way of life and this is also an offshoot of the philosophical heritage of the Jain community. Citing Timberg's observation that most Jains are traders and moneylenders and such occupations have need of community cohesion. Ranu, however, is sceptical about community cohesion affecting voting behaviour. Her appraisal is that the Jains engaged in business and commercial activities are more likely to vote for BJP, which is perceived as a pro-business political party. Most Jains think about the Congress as a party having socialism as its ideology and for that reasons they are likely to shun it considering their *Bania*/trading background. She also firmly establishes the linkage between occupation and political choices by arguing that the Chathuth Jains who do not reside in Gujarat and Rajasthan and are not engaged in business and money lending are not BJP supporters as they vote for different political parties.

The next grouping of papers relates to caste-community comprising two papers. The very mention of caste in the Indian context flashes a social scenario wherein a group of people having advantage of a "godly-ordained" upper caste tag manipulating and abusing the so-called lower castes. The caste system is the most potent apparatus of social exploitation which has religious sanction. Despite a series of reforms of Hindu society and framing and adoption of a democratic-socialist-secular constitution the caste-system as a distinctive attribute of Indian society remains unharmed. It must also be noted that with the exception of the Phule-Ambedkar tradition of social reforms, there is hardly any other significant reformer who espoused complete abolition of the caste system. Most reformers including Gandhi sponsored abolition of untouchability and not the institution of caste. Consequently, the Indian Constitution declares the practice of untouchability as a crime but is silent on the abolition of the caste system.

Murzban Jal emphasises that a new language beyond the realms of caste and class must be created for "the dialectical materialist transcendence of caste" might bring it in altercation with the traditional social order. Jal's paper is more about caste and its impact on socio-political spheres rather than the electoral behaviour of the lower castes. It makes it indispensable as it brings into being a conceptual foundation that helps understand Dalit politics including electoral behaviour explicated in the next two papers. By creating a new language relating to caste he means that the tools of managing caste such as reservations and other programmes purportedly aimed at realisation of social justice have become outdated and a new exemplar is needed.

Jal is of the opinion that caste is to be grasped as 'dialectical essence' for its constantly varying quality. He argues that behind the façade of 'Constitutional Democracy' in India it is caste that manipulates the process of governance and the laws, as they are a throwback of the colonial past, are instruments of repression. Hence, the Constitution too is a kind of repressive implement. He is aware that there are various pretexts of conflicts such as class antagonism, political economy, the state apparatus, cultural diversity and hegemony but the caste battle is the epicentre of all the battles. He laments that neither the left intellectuals nor intellectuals on the right made any attempt to appraise the true complexion of the Indian state that came into being after the end of colonial rule. According to Jal, it is a Patron State that treats its people as clients and not as citizens.

He acknowledges the pivotal role Ambedkar played in critiquing the institution of caste and its deleterious impact on Indian society, politics and economy. Nevertheless, he is not too happy with the post-Ambdkar scholarship which he calls biased and commonplace and which is ineffectual in enervating 'caste and its trauma' that are entrenched in the liberal discourse of Indian democracy.

Jal insists on creation of a new language to critique caste in India because he reasons that in the contemporary scenario, the thought of a revolution is a necessity; it is no more a luxury for the intellectuals. He brings to a close by quoting Žižek, "the very medium of non-violence of mutual recognition, involves unconditional violence."

Dr. Harish Wankhede interprets BJP securing a majority in the Lok Sabha in the 2014 Parliamentary Elections and 2017

Assembly Elections in UP as the efficacy of its strategy of 'divide and rule' of the backward castes' votes. The BJP could successfully mobilise the extremely weaker caste segments in terms of economic and social status within the broad groupings of Dalits and OBCs by propagandising the Hindutva brand of politics among them. A carefully designed strategy was adopted by the Hindu Right by convincing certain caste groups which are at the bottom of socio-economic development that all the benefits offered by the government for the uplift of the Dalits and OBCs were arrogated by already privileged sections among them. This line of propaganda was cleverly clubbed with Hindutva ideology to pitch the extremely marginalised groups against 'Yadav, Jatav and Muslim communities'.

Wankhede points out that the BJP through three-pronged strategy could manage to form a formidable social alliance in its favour. Firstly, BJP exploited the internal hierarchal groupings of the Dalits by intensifying their loathing and misgivings towards each other and in this the processes of modern democracy too contributed because it helped each caste segment to vie for political gains. Secondly, the BJP declared that the reservation policy required necessary reforms because the existing system had helped certain castes like Yadav and Jatav to get all the benefits at the cost of extremely poor and disadvantaged castes. Through a project of sustained propaganda the BJP succeeded in projecting certain Dalit and OBC sections as 'the new middle class'. Thirdly, BJP aggressively put into effect its time-tested stratagem of polarising society on communal lines. Wankhede observes that a sizable section of Dalits and the OBCs continue to be associated with the Hindu practices of idol worshipping, observing local ceremonies and cherishing traditional myths. The RSS volunteers and the BJP workers took advantage of this socio-cultural reality and shrewdly replaced the local cultural folk traditions by Hindutva. This they could do by instigating the marginalised castes against the Muslims on hypersensitive issues like 'cow protection, Ram Temple and of protecting the dignity of Hindu women against the Muslim aggressor (love jihad)'.

In this manner the BJP could build large sections of Dalits and OBCs as its vote bank but did almost nothing for their socio-economic uplift. Wankhede citing a recent study maintains that most members of the Hindu upper middle class continue to be bigoted against the Dalits and the apparent modernism of upper and middle class Hindus is just a veneer. In the Brahminical set of social values and since the institutions of power are controlled by the Hindu upper castes, Dalits and Muslims consistently face violence and humiliations.

In the opening paragraph of the paper, Wankhede expresses hope for the likely alliance of SP-BSP-Congress to challenge the rise of Hindutva politics. However, the alliance could not become a reality because the Congress did not show the inclination. In the concluding part he reiterates that the proposed alliance has to expand its social base by joining hands with the marginalised sections of society 'as equal partners'. Sadly, the three party-alliance could not become a reality and consequences are loud and clear for all to see.

Indian pluralistic society comprises not only religious and caste communities but also the regional communities whose electoral behaviour is guided by the distinctive issues of their regions. Prof. Rasu Chhatrapati Yadav's paper is about the marked difference in voting behaviour of the people of Northern and Southern India. In this context the term region may seem as if it is the admixture of race and region. Rasu believes that the electoral politics of the South is essentially different from that of the North. The first major difference is the presence of strong regional parties in the South. The second distinguishing factor is that the Dalits and backward castes play a dynamic role in the electoral process. The third factor Rasu underscores is that the regional parties of the South respect the value of secularism and accordingly assign 'enough space' to religious minorities in the overall political empowerment.

South India is comparatively peaceful and tolerant in the sense that communal violence rarely raises its ugly head in the states of the South. Since the regional political parties of the South are committed to liberal and secular values they shun Hindutva and in the process have secured the confidence of the religious minorities, in particular, of the Muslims. On account of this, he points out that the literacy rate and educational level in the Southern states is higher than that of the North, the political discourse is mostly confined to the development issues rather than communal political narrative that is the hallmark of North Indian electoral politics. Rasu declares that the regional parties of Southern India have been successful in separating religion from politics which is the basic tenet of a secular state. However, caste is one factor that refuses to disappear from the electoral processes even in the South.

Rasu refers to the machinations of the Hindutva forces to stir the emotions of the majority Hindu community in Kerala over the issue of entry of women into the Sabrimala temple. Despite the Supreme Court's verdict in favour of women's right to enter the temple the Hindutva forces launched protest marches all across the state to badger the CPM government of the state and also to get a foothold for the BJP.

Dr. Noorjahan Momin presents a paper on an aspect of great consequence to the process of electioneering, i.e. the role of media in the contemporary election scenario in India. It must be added that media plays a crucial role in all democracies and its impact on elections can hardly be exaggerated. Dr. Momin points out that the customary role of media as the source of information for the people has altered radically because of globalisation. Media in the current scenario has turned into big business invariably promoting and protecting the interests of those who wield tremendous political and economic power. In the process media itself has become a very powerful institution of contemporary democracies.

She alludes to the pivotal role a partisan media played in the Parliamentary Elections of 2014 that had brought the Hindu nationalist political party, the BJP, to power at the Centre. Having helped BJP acquire the political power, a large section of the Indian media continued to support the BJP in myriad ways. For instance, the failures of the ruling party in matters of governance, law and order and economy have been completely dispensed with. Instead the media devised a strategy to camouflage the political propaganda for the ruling party behind the façade of news and editorial comments. In this manner the media not only managed to create a favourable image for the party in power but also helped the media tycoons acquire incredible power.

She has also commented on the issue of so-called 'development'. In her opinion for this particular project the national economic resources are being transferred to private corporates and it is nothing but a euphemism for open 'loot of state resources'. In support of its policy of privatisation the ruling clique shrewdly cites the 'stipulations' laid down by the World Bank and the IMF for the overall economic reforms. This, Noorjahan points out, has restricted the role of the state while reinforcing the private economic players and lobbyists to make state institutions subservient to push their agenda.

The recent importance attached to the portfolio of communication is primarily, according to her, because of technological advances in the means of communication through which public opinion may be managed in favour of the powers that be. In the new culture of journalism 'strong and independent editors' are passé and editorial boards are no more the decision-makers. Instead all the major decisions are taken by the 'management boards of the media houses'.

Dr. Momin compares the current Indian situation of the business controlled media manipulating state apparatus to campaign for big business houses with that of Russia where such a process began when Yeltsin was facing impediments to be the president for the second time in the presidential elections of 1996. The Russian people were disillusioned because the assured economic prosperity during the break-up of the Soviet Union did not become a reality. Consequently in the subsequent elections for the members of the Duma in 1995, the Communist Party bagged the maximum number of seats. This was alarming for Yeltsin and the big business corporations as a result of which the media was seized by the private business enterprises.

The last two papers relate to the requirement of reforms in the Indian election system to make it more representative of the real aspirations of the people and to involve the maximum number of voters in the electoral process. Dr. Jose George, in order to 'guarantee the success of representative democracy' advocates the reform in the existing electoral system in India. He mentions a few popular systems that are followed in different democracies for choosing the representatives such as, a) the plurality-majority; b) the proportional and c) the semi-proportional. The first one has been in practice in India as well as the UK. Though there are four sub-systems of the plurality-majority, India like the UK adopted the First Past the Post system.

Dr. George has forcefully argued against the First Past the Post system by exposing many of its shortcomings. The major demerit of it is that a candidate elected through such a system, more often than not, does not represent the majority of the electorates. It is because of its innate inadequacies that a candidate who might get 20 per cent of the total valid votes cast sometimes gets elected. Consequently, a party or a coalition of parties that has actually received minority votes may perhaps secure the majority of seats in a legislature. This is obviously the foremost imperfection of the electoral system that is prevalent in the largest democracy of the world. In fact, it is the negation of the spirit of democracy.

Having thus exposed the failings of the FPTP system, Dr. Jose recommends the adoption of the Proportional Representation system. He feels the Proportional Representation system has many advantages such as it might minimise the impact of money power on elections, reduce the role of caste, religion; region, language and so on because the contest will be between the political parties rather than between candidates. Moreover, each vote gets counted and is added up to determine the number of seats a political party is likely to win proportionally. Dr. George believes that through this system democracy gets strengthened. He also points out that the regional parties get better opportunities to have representation in the legislatures depending on their political strength in their respective regions. Thus the central legislature may have an array of various political groups rather than the domination of a single political party. He cautions that the absolute domination of a single political party in the central legislature may lead to authoritarianism as India has witnessed during the internal emergency phase of 1975-1977.

Dr. George has also commented on the Electoral Bonds introduced through the Finance Act 2017 by amending four Acts, viz. the Reserve Bank of India Act of 1914, the Representation of People's Act of 1951, the Income Tax Act of 1961and the Companies Act of 2013. It came into force on January 2, 2018 through which the BJP could augment its financial position so much that other political parties cannot even imagine to match it. According to a report of the *Economic Times*, the BJP was the biggest beneficiary as it could bag almost 95 per cent of the bonds worth more than 210 crores. Dr. George accuses the BJP of manipulation and fraud as the Bill about the electoral bonds was passed as a Money Bill even though it did not qualify to be so under Article 110. It was deliberately done to circumvent the Rajya Sabha where the saffron party did not have the majority support.

The other paper that suggests reforms in India's electoral system with the purpose of increasing the participation of voters in various elections was presented by Dr. Rohidas Munde. He rightly argues that the low percentage of voters in the election is a major area of concern as it mutilates the meaning of true democracy. He identifies the group of voters which usually avoid casting votes. For instance, he points out that "the so-called intellectuals, academicians, policy makers, traders, educated youths" who matter the most commonly eschew voting. He feels if these groups of electorates start casting their votes the Indian legislatures will certainly have better representatives. It may also restrict the candidates with criminal records entering the august law making bodies. Additionally, Dr. Munde feels the impact of big money and muscle power will also be minimised if the necessary reforms are brought about in the existing electoral system in India.

The most desirable reform that he recommends is the use of technology in increasing the percentage of voters. He comments that the Parliamentary Elections of 2014, were significant because for the first time various devices of technology such as Facebook,

Email, SMS, Twitter and 3D were extensively used to influence the voters. Despite this, he laments there was hardly any perceptible increase in voters' turnout Basing his observation on the data from the First General Elections of 1951 to the Sixteenth General Election of 2014, Dr. Munde recapitulates that the average voting percentage did not go beyond 60. This is proof enough of the failure of various efforts that are employed to improve participation of voters.

In order to overcome this serious imperfection of our electoral system, Dr. Munde recommends the use of Internet and cellular phones to be used as voting devices. He rightly points out that since these technological tools are widely used by Indians for varied purposes then there is no harm using them for electoral purposes. If Internet and cellular phones are introduced for casting of votes, Dr. Munde believes that the voting percentage will shoot up to 80-85. He is aware of the possible objections that may be raised by the naysayers to the induction of these technological tools on grounds of safety and secrecy. In response he argues that objections do exist for the use of Electronic Voting Machine (EVM) but the Election Commission did not scrap it. To allay the fears of the objecting parties the Voter Verifiable Paper Audit Trial Machine (VVPATM) was latched to the EVM. He, therefore, argues that in order to ensure safety and secrecy of the voting processes some other technological device may be used. Instead of rejecting technology, the Election Commission of India must introduce the usage of Internet and cellular phones for voting first on an experimental basis. If glitches are noticed they may be rectified technologically. His focal point is that the voting percentage must be improved for strengthening democracy and for that reason we must not shy away from effective technology.

Since the conference in which these papers were presented was held in January 2019, and the process of selection and editing of the papers got completed a few months later, the issues that played a crucial role in the Sixteenth Parliamentary Elections and their impact were not commented upon by scholars. By the time the manuscript was finalised to be handed over to the press, the results of the elections were announced on May 23 with the BJP again emerging as the majority party in the Lower House of Parliament with a few more seats than it bagged in 2014. I, therefore, suggested to the contributing scholars to add brief postscripts to their papers commenting on whether the results of the Sixteenth Parliamentary Elections synchronise with the basic thrust of their respective papers or they cast off the crux of their papers. I am glad that the scholars took note of my request and added postscripts to their papers. In this manner their analyses of different facets of Indian elections have been updated.

Theme

1

Democracy, Electoral Behaviour and Communities as Vote Banks: A Perspective on the Indian Electoral Process

K. Srinivasulu

The history of the post-colonial Indian political system with a democratic framework has been quite complex and exciting. If periodic elections characterise its formal democratic adherence then the trajectory of political electoral participation marks the real test of its substantive democratic content. This raises questions about the nature and quality of political-electoral participation central to it, i.e. how people vote in the elections?

Do they vote as individual citizens or members of larger collectives? Are these collectives/groups ascribed or achieved and self-directed or other-directed? Are these collectives singular or overlapping pluralities? How have they shaped the identities of voters? What is the relationship between the identity as a voter, citizen, member of work space/productive process or as a worker, as a member of a community/group, for example, of a caste, class and religion? What factors influence/activate identities as a result of which identity becomes decisive and under what conditions? Associated are the questions of why, how and whom of the electoral behaviour of these collectives and their voting preferences.

Formally a voter exercising his or her franchise under a constitutional framework is pre-eminently a citizen expected to vote for a party which is evaluated/tested on the basis of its ideology, policy framework, organisation, leadership commitment and ability to protect the country and welfare of the citizens in accordance with the law of the land. Equally, the political parties are expected to appeal to the citizens within the constitutional framework and if elected act within that framework.

What ought to bind a political party and citizen-voter is the sense of *constitutional morality*–the foundational ethic of the Indian state and politics arrived at on the basis of a social contract. Between the high ideal of constitutional morality and the real world of politics there could be a variety of issues, gaps and tensions. Significantly, they could be seen related to what can be called the *translatability* problem involving political language, concepts, ideas, images, metaphors, across various actors–citizens, parties, leaders, ideologues, media, bureaucracy, intellectuals, judiciary, etc. In other words, the huge institutional and non-institutional, formal and informal sites, edifices, interactions and processes that involve state and non-state actors and stakeholders need to be factored in to understand the electoral democratic process.

There could be noticed, as diagnosed, alerted and commented upon by Babasaheb Ambedkar in his last speech, 'Life of Contradictions' to the Constituent Assembly, "a contradiction, asymmetry and tension between the constitutional framework that accords equal value–one person, one vote–in the political domain and the absence, in fact denial of it (one person, one value) in the social and economic domain. It is this mismatch between the constitutionally accorded formal and political equality and existing social and economic inequality manifest principally in the caste system that becomes a major hurdle in the creation of a democratic, egalitarian and just society in India."

If the constitutional ideal and its translation into reality is one major challenge that has paved the way for the tensions and conflicts between the upper caste and dominant social classes on the one hand and the subaltern caste/classes–particularly the Dalits -

on the other; these conflicts have not been fought in the domain of electoral politics alone. In fact, electoral politics being dominated by the dominant caste led political formations–national parties led by Brahminical and regional parties by dominant regional peasant castes in different states–often obfuscate and camouflage the real contradictions rather than addressing them and resolving them. As a result, these contradictions spill over to the non-electoral domains and spheres of civil and subaltern societies.

India has been witness to non-electoral mass mobilisations that sought to correct the inadequacies of the dominant party and electoral system (for example, JP and Anna movements) and anti-systemic movement (like the Naxalite movement). The understanding of the electoral politics and the dynamics of mobilisation would be inadequate without a critical consideration of these social and political articulations.

At another level India's democratic experiment has brought an important facet of Indian politics to the surface which has not been paid adequate analytical and conceptual attention. It is related to the political ideology and language of electoral democracy in India. This language could be seen crossing the limits of and often violating the liberal lexicon of politics and language of rights that the Indian Constitution is embedded in.[1] One aspect of this is the change in the language of rights from individual to community rights and increasing articulation of community rights and idiom of communal politicisation and mobilisation. This change needless to say has an impact on electoral slogans, issues and of course mobilisation.

This problematic could be captured in terms of the tension between *'-etic' categories* of liberal constitutional politics and the highly diverse *'-emic' notions* that are rooted in the historical diversity and have evolved with variations along macro-micro, western-indigenous and the complex linguistic-regional differences and caste/class dynamics. There is a growing anxiety among the political elite and an opportunity for self-expression and source of identity formation for the subaltern communities. But what is clearly visible is the problem of translatability in terms of concepts, aspirations, expressions, solidarities and community formations on the one hand and 'incommensurability' of institutional patterns, protocols and official and non-official interactions and elite-subaltern expectations on the other.[2]

In terms of conceptual language, the Indian political mosaic presents quite a complex scenario ridden with flourish, differences, tensions, even conflicts: if the Constitution speaks the liberal language of rights, equality and justice, then the Hindutva project has brought in the high Sanskritic conceptual apparatus of dharma, raja dharma, karma, artha and punya. The subaltern caste political universe is rich with the new indigenous emic categories of Bahujan, Dalit, achyuth, shoshan, samajik nyaya-anyaya, etc.

These different political languages/idioms not merely express terminological differences but in fact symbolise contrasting political imaginaries and point to deep cosmological fault lines in Indian politics that defy received frames of analysis, easy solutions and promise to get intensified in the formation of community identities that pose a challenge to the ethnography and influence the sociology of Indian electoral democracy.

The study of electoral behaviour in India has largely been dominated by empiricism–who voted for whom, which party, why and for what reasons. The dominant stimulus-response model followed to collect information about voters' choices, preferences along party, candidate and policy lines, the respondents identified with their preferences in terms of caste, class, age and gender. This exercise undertaken in the behavioural-empirical tradition is certainly useful to feel the pulse of the people. But it only treats people as voters, as an embodiment of sense data. What is definitely not captured is the deeper ideological transformation that underlines the electoral political change. For this, we need to treat people at different levels–as voters, citizens, as members of variegated civil and political society, as members of different communities–caste class and religious groups, and as capable of intellectual abilities to think and take decisions in the Gramscian sense.

The plea is that, to understand the electoral behaviour of Indian voters we need to go beyond appearances and explore the subterraneous transformation that needs deeper engagement with the geometry of identity formation–fluidity, variation, change and difference and sameness or unity and their varying temporal, spatial and social markers.

I

To map this process we could identify certain markers–the significant ones being–region, caste, class, gender, community, etc. These identity markers needless to state are neither universal nor static. Instead, they have to be understood and evaluated along the temporal, contextual and sociological axes.

Since the focus of this presentation is on the question of communities in relation to electoral politics and processes, it would be instructive to reflect on the concept of community. The two significant sociological concepts of *gemeinschaft* and *gesellschaft*[3] capture two distinct modes of individuals relating to each other seen in a historical process. They are helpful to perspectives the question of community identity and political dynamics. While *gemeinschaft* refers to a social structure where relations between individuals are bonded into a close community based on personal and familial ties, in contrast, *gesellschaft* connotes a change to explicitly individualised, impersonal relations. Instead of positing them in a dichotomous mode if these concepts are seen as meant to capture the transition from the traditional feudal to a market oriented transactional capitalist society based on impersonal ties, they would serve a better analytical purpose.

When the concept of community is defined as a collectivity what become critical to it are the following aspects: i) identity based on sharing and commonality ii) solidarity; iii) possibility of collective decision and action. Concept of community could be characterised as an experiential/empirical one and it could also be used to refer to an imagined possibility that could go beyond the empirical. For instance, if Mahar and Mang are empirical terms that refer to concrete castes/caste clusters, then the concept of Dalit is an abstract non-empirical one that is more to be imagined and acted upon to forge solidarity on a higher plane and for a higher perhaps distant goal.

An empirical community could be defined as an immediate, experiential, face-to-face and primordial one where membership is almost natural and by birth like in the case of caste, religion, language and region. The loyalty to it is emotive and primordial almost taken for granted and its weakening could only happen as a result of a conscious political decision and disruptive action. Caste is a classic example of such a community where membership and identity is by birth. Caste in the pre-modern period was a localised fuzzy identity with no clear or definite numerical strength and spatial sense of solidarity. It is with the onset of colonial modernity, new identities started taking shape and assumed effectiveness in Indian society. With this caste also got modernised and could no longer be said to be a fuzzy entity.

It is with the census, an important instrumentality of the modern state for counting and controlling its citizenry, introduced by the colonial state in India that caste became an enumerated category and number became the basis of interest articulation, aggregation, empowerment and even manipulation. Caste which was a thing-in-itself with a fuzzy existence in the pre-colonial India could assume a clear form and emerge as a predominant marker by transforming into caste-for-itself. Caste acquiring enumerability could become an instrument of social and political action over a temporal frame and spatial terrain: it is evident from the consolidation of caste identities through associations and rise of caste movements demanding self-respect, equality and justice.

An imagined community[4] in contrast is a collective based on an idea or vision expanded temporally and spatially effecting the feeling of a shared identity and a solidarity forged trans-empirically through ideation to achieve certain social or political aims. The veracity and durability of such an identity would depend on the coherence and vitality of the ideology that informs it. Since identity is contextual and dynamic there could be identified two possibilities. One, there could be inter-sectionality between identities giving rise to the presence of plural communities in which a person could be a member with differential priority and sense of belonging and in the event of multiple community identities and membership–one could be weak or strong; and two, when the community is seen as weakening or non-viable or irrelevant one could shift one's loyalty and eventually exit from it thereby rendering it superfluous[5]. Like in the case of an empirical community even an imagined community could be forged on the basis of different identities: linguistic, caste, religious, cultural, economic, etc. but needs to be deeply engaged with and impacted by a strong commitment.

II

The concept of a vote-bank in the context of electoral democracy in India, seen in the background of the above discussion, can be defined as a *bloc* of voters from a single community or cluster of communities, natural or socially forged on identity of interests, assumed or felt, who owe their loyalty to a candidate or political party and express it through their support to them during elections with a certain consistency and expectant durability. It is presumed that a vote-bank is forged on the expectation of returns for the loyalty and delivery of community votes to a party. The vehicle of this often is the community leader who plays a mediator with a party or candidate. The latter as a patron exercises influence on the voters as clients. In other words, the concept of the vote-bank is based on the patron-client relationship and through persistence it seeks to reinforce itself. Needless to state, vote-banks in India are forged on caste, religious, sub-regional and linguistic identities. The situation of a community, because of its minority status or social insecurity or economic vulnerability often becomes the basis for converting it into a stable vote-bank for a party in lieu of its promise to alleviate its problems and stand by it.[6]

Nonetheless, the question is: how and what has been the trajectory of the vote-bank both as an idea or concept and as a concrete phenomenon during the seven decades of our post-independence democratic politics. To make sense of this we need to map the trajectory of Indian electoral democracy by examining the changes in the party system, the terms of discourse and appeal and even social movements which are indicators of the changing people's perceptions and aspirations. It is pertinent to note the importance of political regimes in influencing/shaping/reinforcing identities and therefore the fate of the vote-bank as the basis of electoral mobilisation.

To do this the best strategy would be to begin with a periodisation of Indian politics. Broadly, the following phases could be identified on the basis of political, discursive and organisational shifts in Indian politics.

I. Phase of Congress Dominance: 1947-1967
II. Challenges to Congress leading to the Emergency: 1968-1977
III. Post-Emergency Phase: 1978-1988
IV. Post-Congress Phase: 1989-2004
V. Congress Come-back: 2004-2014
VI. BJP Dominance: 2014-

The first two decades of independence are the period of the dominance of Congress during which it acted more as a system (*a la* Rajni Kothari[7]) rather than as a party. This was a period which saw a prioritisation of the nation-building and state-building as challenges before the country. The most daunting challenge was to forge a sense of participation and ownership in this process. The dominant narrative of this phase could be termed as 'Nationisation of Indian politics'. The study of Indian politics (for instance, by scholars like Morris-Jones and Rajni Kothari[8]) of this period viewed India from above with nation, Centre and all India as the vantage point and region, province and state seen as secondary, dependent and derivative in terms of methodological premise as well as ontological priority.

This was also a period when India was discovering its own self as an electoral democracy by bringing in people to participate in the electoral process as voters, as party cadres and leaders and mobilisers of electoral support. What is found to be a convenient platform for the mobilisation of popular support was the pre-existing traditional social structures like caste, tribe, religion which were found to be useful formats to mobilise people. In the political and electoral scenario they got recognition and were useful as instruments of the electoral mobilisation.

Logic of Regionalisation of Indian Politics

The assertion of regional identities in Indian politics can be said to have started with the coming to power of the non-Congress governments in the late 1960s. The Emergency in a significant sense gave a further fillip to the assertion and consolidation of regional identities as evident from the fact of the rise of regional party formations in almost all the states. In view of this, the coming back to power of the Congress at the Centre in 1980 cannot be read as the reassertion of a national party over the prevailing regional assertions. Instead, as Rudolphs[9] remarked, the Congress comeback was not a 'restoration' of the party but a simple return of it to power.

To cut a long story short, the government formation at the Centre since has seen the crucial, in fact, central strategic role of the regional parties regardless of the alliance being pre-poll or post-poll. The formation of NDA and UPA or the explicit talk now of 'federal front' (or third front) highlights the criticality of regional parties in Indian politics and government formation at the national level.

The political scenario in Indian states can be captured by identifying the following patterns of electoral-political contestations:

I. States where there is a direct contest between the Congress and the BJP (Gujarat, Rajasthan, MP) the Congress and the CPI(M) (Kerala)

II. States where there is a contest between the Congress and a regional party (Telangana)

III. States where there is a contest between the BJP and a regional party (North-East)

IV. States where there is a contest between two or more regional parties (Andhra Pradesh)

V. States where there is a contest with the national parties in alliance with regional parties (Tamil Nadu, Maharashtra)

VI. States where there is a multi-cornered contest involving both national and regional parties (Karnataka)

This *logic of regionalisation* of Indian politics has an important bearing on the electoral politics and the strategies of mobilisation and vote bank as a concept needs to be re-examined in this context and the ensuing intense competition, polarisation and opposition. One can no longer talk about communities as vote banks in the sense in which they could be in the earlier decades.

What characterise the present political context are:

(i) A sharp social polarisation along caste and religious fault lines (Lingalyat vs Volaligas)
(ii) Political mobilisation is sought to be effected through long-term social/religious mobilisation (Lingayats)
(iii) Communities are sought to be pitted against each other for electoral mobilisation (Madiga vs. Mala)
(iv) This polarisation is not static; through various means (through alliances) inter-sectional solidarity is sought to be forged.

What is analytically useful is to identify the underlying logic of India's post-independence political history as reflected in the above analysis. One, the vision of India from above and macro—all-India/ Centre as the point of departure. Two, is a view of India as a nation of multiple linguistic regions. This can be called regionalisation or federalisation of Indian politics.

III

There is a visible contradictory development in Indian politics that is pertinent to understand the dynamics of electoral politics. One is the emergence of civil and subaltern societies (*a la* Gramsci) as active sites of self-mobilisation and politicisation and the other is the oligarchic nature of leadership of regional parties with power vested in the El Supremo of the party, his family and close coterie (often on caste lines). This raises an important question: How do the personalisation/centralisation of decision-making and power become possible and sustainable in the context of heightened and decentralised community assertion and mobilisation?

Electoral campaigns have seen an increasing populist personalisation of appeal to the electorate by the Supremo (for example, KCR in the recent Telangana elections). How does this impact on the patron-client relations implicit in the vote bank format?

Indian elections in the last few decades have seen a phenomenal increase in money power in the form of electoral spending. It is said that the electoral domain has been converted into a marketplace where voters have been treated as purchase-able and have in fact got commoditised. This raises the questions: what has been the impact of electoral spending and implicit commodification of votes on the community-centric vote bank politics? And what are its implications for the future of democratic participation?

It is important to consider the above questions to understand the dynamics of community behaviour especially in relation to elections.

IV

Any analysis of electoral politics would be incomplete without a reference to the larger macro context of India's political economy. Liberalisation of the Indian economy since the 1990s has led to the dispossession, displacement and loss of livelihood of vast sections of popular classes, the process of primitive accumulation fastened and intensified by the neo-liberal policies has led to crisis of the agrarian, traditional artisanal and occupational communities and small producers and unorganised services and businesses by dispossessing them of their means of livelihood.[10]

This raises two important questions:

1. How have these communities as victims of primitive accumulation responded to this process? What has been the nature of response in terms of solidarity, mobilisation and participation in elections?
2. How is the crisis of such a magnitude, intensity and scale sought to be addressed by the political parties/regimes to sustain and re-orient their support base in the electoral domain? In other words, how have they sought to offset "the effects of primitive accumulation" experienced by the popular classes?

The point of divergence and convergence between these two contradictory processes is crucial in any serious scholarly analysis of electoral support of political parties and the basis on which support is sought and consolidated. When communities as occupational castes–as peasant, artisanal and service and labour castes–are adversely affected do they continue to support as such castes or as some other identity groups?

It would be instructive to visit the debate around the concept of political society initiated by Partha Chatterjee. Differentiating the concept of civil society widely used in Indian social science analyses from political society, Chatterjee seeks to address the paradox of Indian electoral democracy. For him, while civil society refers to the urban middle class as "the sphere that seeks to be congruent with the normative models of bourgeois civil society and represents the domain of capitalist hegemony", political society comprises "large sections of rural population and urban poor" who "make their claims on government, and in turn are governed, not within the framework of stable constitutionally defined rights and laws, but rather through temporary, contextual and unstable arrangements arrived at through direct political negotiations".[11] The concept of civil society is attributed limited analytical potential to understand politics in India because of the predominant middle class marker on it and for the non-inclusion of the marginalised and dispossessed subaltern communities as their interests and aspirations fall outside the domain of civil society.

Chatterjee analytically deploys the concept of political society as a sphere that facilitates mediation with subaltern society by dominant parties/regimes to address the challenges increasingly posed with respect to the support of subaltern class-castes. In the context of neo-liberal policy dispensation which has led to the displacement, dispossession and loss of livelihoods of the vast majority of people as a fall-out of heightened primitive accumulation the powers-that-be have experienced a demonstrated crisis of legitimacy.

In this context, in Chatterjee's view, the concept of political society is seen as having the explanatory possibility to address the problem of popular consent. Thus, political society is seen as the domain that facilitates the liberalising regime to initiate populist *welfarist* policies and schemes to contain popular discontent and meet their expectations and garner their electoral support by lessening if not eliminating the effects of pro-corporate policy turn resulting in the process of dispossession of popular classes from their means of livelihood and their displacement from their habitats.[12]

V

In the political history of post-independence India, the Emergency marks a major watershed. Two major developments witnessed in the post-Emergency period have consequences for electoral politics. One, the gradual and definite *expansion of popular political participation in the electoral and non-electoral domains*–as evident in the increasing electoral turn-out, emergence of different issue-based social movements, expansion of civil and democratic rights movements and rise of identity-based mobilisation. Two, the *regionalisation of Indian politics* as evident in the rise of regional parties in different state theatres and the consolidation of regional dominant caste/classes as powerful political forces and their continuous negotiation with the subaltern castes in a variety of ways to forge winnable social alliances. The last two decades of politics is also witness to the fact that the subalterns cannot be taken for granted by the political parties and there is a need to continuously pay attention to them and address their concerns. This is clear from the unpredictability and precariousness of political parties, frequent alternation of power between parties in each successive election and the narrowing of the electoral margins between contending parties or their alliances. This scenario marks a decisive shift in the strategic position of the subaltern groups *vis-à-vis* the political society.

It is true that political parties, given the phenomenal self-assertion by the subaltern communities, have floated respective caste associations as party affiliates and in the process projected their own party loyalists as community leaders or co-opted the leaders who have emerged through the autonomous churning in the subaltern activity and self-mobilisation with the promises of accommodation, enticement or even coercion, so that the possibility of and space for an independent subaltern voice is either rendered ineffective or presented as consistent with the dominant discourse. It is undoubtedly a significant trend in contemporary Indian politics that the autonomous spheres of the subaltern and civil society have been co-opted, moderated, sanitised and stripped of autonomy and thus sought to be reduced considerably and rendered ineffective. This undoubtedly has a bearing on their community behaviour and collective electoral participation.

The electoral studies empirically inclined, as they are, do not tend to address the possibility of subaltern autonomy which has to be addressed theoretically. It is the openness on the conceptual side that makes the possibility of alternatives conceivable and accessible. As suggested earlier there has been a marked assertion of identity and autonomy among the subaltern castes, especially in the post-Emergency period. Given the volatility implicit in the assertion parties have increasingly found themselves in an uneasy position to negotiate with this subaltern reality. It is necessary to note in this context Ambedkar's observation that caste is not only division of labour but also division of labourers. If caste can be a potential unifier given a powerful imagination and imagery in empirical actuality it is predominantly a marker of division and conflict. This has come in handy to the dominant castes to use caste as a platform for divide and garner support electoral strategy. As a result the dominant political interests have found it easy and comfortable and therefore sought to use the internal divisions among the subaltern castes. The Scheduled Castes' sub-categorisation is a classic case which was used effectively to perpetuate fragmentation among the Dalits on caste lines and thereby render them politically ineffective.

The analysis of subaltern politics clearly illustrates that these communities have shown a high level of awareness of their rights in the framework of the Constitution and law and have pragmatically articulated their demands in the language of rights, equality and justice. The subaltern social movements in the decades subsequent to the Emergency as part of the heightened civil rights assertion catalysed by the anti-Emergency spirit have demonstrated a dual nature: they not only fought against the injustices perpetuated by the dominant caste-classes but also exposed and questioned the illegality of the state, especially atrocities committed by the law and order machinery and dislocation and displacement caused in the name of development. This undoubtedly has assumed phenomenal proportions, though largely localised and issue-based, in the post-liberalisation period as a result of the neoliberal reforms.

The following changes induced by the dominant caste led political society have to be considered theoretically and practically in analysing the role of communities as vote banks:

(i) Attempts at the co-option of the activists into the mainstream party structures albeit in subaltern positions. This is sought to be pursued through the caste cells (SC, ST and BC cells) by political parties and by the NGOs though their funded voluntary activities.

(ii) Intensification of the internal differences among the castes and movements to further divisions and disunity so that we would not pose a threat to the dominant structures; widening differences have, as the Madiga experience shows, has rendered them ineffective.

(iii) Strategic primacy to the middle class issues in terms of discursive priority and policy attention have rendered substantive subaltern (Dalit) anxieties, aspirations and demands insignificant, if not invisible in the political and public policy domain.

(iv) The gap between the caste elite and working masses widening, the visible elite non-response or even indifference to the problems of the lower classes within the subaltern community reflects the objective class differentiation within the subaltern communities on the one hand, and ideological distance in the political domain on the other. The absence of a conscious engagement with this reality has been used by the dominant parties for electoral gains and for continued social engineering.

The above changes in the subaltern society and politics reflect the strategic ascendancy of dominant political society in contemporary India. This in fact reinforces subordination of the lower castes to the dominant castes in the political sphere making them vote banks rather than autonomous actors in electoral politics making their own choices and .becoming participants in the governance process.

Postscript

The 2019 election marks a departure in terms of the nature of competition, shaping and projection of issues and shifts in electoral support base. In a significant sense, each election is different in terms of political and social character. The social kaleidoscope of electoral shifts in 2019 has to be analysed in relation to the changed context that raised serious questions regarding the role of governmental and non-governmental institutions and processes like, for instance, the Election Commission and media, the visibly weak and fragmented nature of civil society, and uneven endowment of the parties in terms of their access to resources, media time and opportunities to reach out to their social constituencies.

What marked the central rallying point in this election is the concern with the national security. With the national identity and integrity emerging as the dominant narrative all other narratives sought to be forged on the planks of the agrarian and rural well being, the issue of employment, the question of federal devolution and states' autonomy that dominated Indian electoral narratives in the post-Emergency period more so since the introduction of neo-liberal reforms in the 1990s, have taken a back seat. The BJP's grand narrative of 'nation in peril' that dominated the electoral campaign in the north and the west supported by well-crafted political and social coalitions could be seen disturbing and even damaging the evolved and time-tested regional/local configurations in different states. The electoral outcome nevertheless demonstrates a schism that sets the south Indian states of Andhra Pradesh, Telangana and Tamil Nadu as the strong bastions of regional parties. The physiognomy and future of Indian democracy going by these signals could be in for far-reaching changes.

Notes

1. Some of these issues are discussed by Ashis Nandy. See his, 'The Culture of Indian Politics: A Stock Taking' in *The Journal of Asian Studies*, Vol. 30, No. 1 (1970), pp. 57-79. Also, 'The Political Culture of the Indian State' in *Dedalus*, Vol. 118, No. 4 (1989), pp. 1-26.
2. For a discussion on this issue in a different analytical mode, see, Satish Saberwal (1996), *Roots of Crisis: Interpreting Contemporary Indian Society*, OUP, Delhi.
3. Ferdinand van Tonnies (2001), *Community and Civil Society*, Cambridge University Press, Cambridge.
4. For an elaboration of this idea see, Benedict Anderson (1991), *Imagined Communities: Reflections on the Origin and Spread of Nationalism*, Verso, London.
5. Albert O. Hirschman (1970), *Exit, Voice and Loyalty: Responses to Decline in Firms, Organizations and States*, Harvard University Press.
6. For an early analysis of the concept and its empirical deployment, see, M.N. Srinivas (1995), 'The Social System of a Mysore Village' in *Social Change in Modern India*, Orient BlackSwan; and F.G. Bailey (1963), *Politics and Social Change*, OUP.
7. Rajni Kothari (1964), 'The Congress "System" in India', *Asian Survey*, Vol. 4, No. 12, December.
8. W.H. Morris-Jones (1971), *Government and Politics of India*, Hutchinson, London; Rajni Kothari (2012), *Politics in India*, Orient BlackSwan, Hyderabad.
9. Lloyd I. Rudolph and Susanne H. Rudolph (1981), 'Transformation of Congress Party–Why 1980 Was Not a Restoration', *Economic and Political Weekly*, May 2, Vol. 16, Issue No. 18.
10. For an analysis of this process through the case of SEZs see, K. Srinivasulu (2014), 'Land Acquisition and Popular Resistance: Politics of Special Economic Zones in Andhra Pradesh', Rob Jenkins, Lorraine Kennedy, and Partha Mukhopadhyay (eds.), *The Politics of Special Economic Zones in India*, Oxford University Press, Delhi.
11. Partha Chatterjee (2008), 'Democracy and Economic Transformation in India', *Economic and Political Weekly*, April 19,

p. 57. It is reproduced in Partha Chatterjee (2011), *Lineages of Political Society,* Permanent Black, Ranikhet.

12. The concepts of civil and political society are central to the Gramscian theoretical discourse. It is sufficient to note in the context of the present discussion that there are serious variations in the deployment of these concepts in Chatterjee from that of the Gramscian provenance. For a critical discussion on Chatterjee's position see, Srinivasulu (2019), 'Political Society, Caste Dominance and Subaltern Society: Reflecting on the Modes of Engagement with the Dalit Subalternity' in Ashok Pankaj and Ajit Pandey (eds.) (2019), *Dalits, Subalternity and Social Change in India,* Routledge, London.

References

Anderson, Benedict (1991). *Imagined Communities: Reflections on the Origin and Spread of Nationalism,* Verso, London.

Balagopal, K. (2000), 'A Tangled Web: Subdivision of SC Reservations in AP', *Economic and Political Weekly,* March 25-31.

Bardhan, P. (1998), *The Political Economy of Development in India*, OUP, Delhi.

Chatterjee, Partha (2008), 'Democracy and Economic Transformation in India', *Economic and Political Weekly*, April 19. It is reproduced in Partha Chatterjee (2011): *Lineages of Political Society*, Permanent Black, Ranikhet.

Gramsci, A. (1971), *Selections from Prison Notebooks*, edited and translated by Quintin Hoare and Geoffrey Nowell Smith, Lawrence and Wishart, London.

Hyderabad Political Economy Group (2012), 'Laxmipet Dalit Killings', *Economic and Political Weekly*, December 1.

Sarkar, Sumit (1997), *Writing Social History*, Oxford University Press, Delhi.

Srinivasulu, K. (2002), 'Caste, Class and Social Articulation in Andhra Pradesh: Mapping Differential Regional Trajectories,' *ODI* Working Paper 179.

Srinivasulu, K. (2014), 'Land Acquisition and Popular Resistance: Politics of Special Economic Zones in Andhra Pradesh', Rob Jenkins, Lorraine Kennedy, and Partha Mukhopadhyay (eds.), *The Politics of Special Economic Zones in India,* Oxford University Press, Delhi.

Srinivasulu, K. (2019), 'Political Society, Caste Dominance and Subaltern Society: Reflecting on the Modes of Engagement with the Dalit Subalternity' in Ashok K. Pankaj and Ajit Pandey (eds.) (2019), *Dalits, Subalternity and Social Change in India,* Routledge, London.

Religion

2

Muslim Voting Behaviour: Myth and Reality

Zaheer Ali

> Democracy is a system where people are counted not weighed.
>
> *–Muhammad Iqbal*

> It was the first religion that preached and practised democracy; for, in the mosque, when the call for prayer is sounded and worshippers are gathered together, the democracy of Islam is embodied five times a day when the peasant and king kneel side by side and proclaim: 'God Alone is Great'...
>
> *–Sarojini Naidu*

According to the 2011 Census of India, 1.80 million people or more than 14 per cent of India's population (roughly 172 million people) have declared themselves to be the adherents of Islam[1]. It must, nonetheless be underscored that Muslims in India do not constitute an absolute social category. They are as heterogeneous as Indian society is. Contrary to popular perception and the claims of the Muslim clerics, Muslims in India are divided on caste, language, region, ethnicity and even racial lines. It must, therefore, be clear that despite the hype created by the mainstream media the Indian Muslims do not constitute a vote bank because their voting behaviour across the country is far from being identical.

Understandably, in view of the social reality, the Muslim voting behaviour differs from caste to caste, language to language, region to region and so on.

Secondly, the Muslim voting pattern has undergone sweeping changes during the last seventy years of the Indian republic. In this chapter the reflections on Muslim voting behaviour are mainly confined to the Parliamentary elections. The changing pattern of Muslim voting may be classified into three major phases. They are:

1. The security-engendered phase of almost en bloc voting. (1951-1977)
2. The coming-of-age phase of political self-assurance. (1977-1989)
3. The Strategic Voting phase. (1989-present)

I. The Security-Engendered Phase (1951-1977)

The partition of the country was a watershed in the history of the Muslims in India. It has been explained time and again that the movement for a separate homeland for the Muslims in the form of Pakistan was not a movement of the Muslims but it was conceived, carried out and accomplished by a microscopic section of the landlords and elite of North India and in the later phase the Muslim business class of Mumbai. The overwhelming majority of Muslims, the bulk of whom comprised weavers, tanners, cobblers, scavengers, carpenters, butchers, fishermen, masons, utensil makers, artisans, petty businessmen, agriculture workers and unskilled labourers did not have any role to play in the movement driven by the infamous 'two-nation-theory'. The irony, however, was that most of the common Muslims who had nothing to do with Pakistan and preferred to stay back in the land where their ancestors lived for centuries and buried, had to face the wrath of the Hindu Right immediately after the partition of the country mainly led by the Hindu Mahasabha, the RSS and also a section of the Indian National Congress.

The mention of the Congress along with the Mahasabha and the RSS should not be a surprise because the INC right from its inception had been ideologically an eclectic organisation wherein the Hindu hardliners constituted a sizable and potent section. Immediately after independence, Sardar Vallabhbhai Patel, in a speech delivered at Lucknow menacingly warned the Muslims that simply because they stayed back in India for whatever reason would not suffice but they would have to do 'much more' to prove their loyalty towards the country. In 1948 itself the Home Ministry under Patel secretly sent out a secret circular to all the ministries stating that the Muslim employees posed a serious threat to national security as "it is obvious that they (Muslim employees) constitute a dangerous element in the fabric of administration; and it is essential that they should not be entrusted with any confidential or secret work or allowed to hold key posts."[2] Patel died in 1950 but the anti-Muslim circular remained in force till 1969, which means that all through the Nehru years and beyond, Muslims were officially discriminated against in public services. No wonder Narendra Modi is an unwavering supporter of Patel.

Consequently, the Muslims in Northern India were forced to live with a guilt complex as the Hindu Right would constantly blame them for the partition of the country. They were devastatingly poor, most of them without proper education, bereft of business means and acumen, no hope of public or private employment, partly because of lack of qualifications and chiefly because of discrimination against them particularly in the public sector. In short, a huge section of them was reduced to the level of beggars. The constant harassment by communal forces and the biased police had rendered most of them hopeless and fatalistic. Many of them had lost the will to fight back and survive. At this critical juncture, the leadership of Maulana Abul Kalam Azad played the most crucial role. Azad was a senior and much respected leader of the Congress. He had served as the President of the Congress seven times and during the most crucial period immediately before the independence of India he was President of the Congress continuously for six years, i.e. from 1940 to 1946. He was violently opposed to the reprehensible 'two-nation-theory' and was the only stalwart leader who never accepted partition of the country.

He was aware that a section of the Indian Muslims misguided by the charismatic leadership of Jinnah did oppose him during the heydays of the freedom struggle. Nonetheless, he was astute enough to appraise the plight of Indian Muslims, most of whom had nothing to do with Pakistan. He rose to the occasion to give moral support and inspiration to the hapless lot of the Muslims by instilling confidence among them that India was as much a nation of the Muslims as it was that of the Hindus. Following the afternoon prayer of a Friday on October 23, 1947, Azad addressed the huge Muslim congregation in the historic Jama Masjid of Delhi Consider a few excerpts:

> My brethren,
>
> You know what has brought me here today. This congregation at Shah Jahan's historic mosque is not an unfamiliar sight for me. Here, I have addressed you on several previous occasions. Since then we have seen many ups and downs. At that time, instead of weariness, your faces reflected serenity, and your hearts, instead of misgivings, exuded confidence. The uneasiness on your faces and the desolation in your hearts that I see today, reminds me of the events of the past few years.
>
> Do you remember? I hailed you, you cut off my tongue; I picked my pen, you severed my hand; I wanted to move forward, you broke off my legs; I tried to run, and you injured my back. When the bitter political games of the last seven years were at their peak, I tried to wake you up at every danger signal. You not only ignored my call but revived all the past traditions of neglect and denial. As a result the same perils surround you today, whose onset had previously diverted you from the righteous path....
>
> Now that Indian politics has taken a new direction, there is no place in it for the Muslim League. Now the question is whether or not we are capable of constructive thinking. For this, I have invited the Muslim leaders of India to Delhi, during the second week of November....
>
> Where are you going and why? Raise your eyes. The minarets of Jama Masjid want to ask you a question. Where have you lost the glorious pages from your chronicles? Was it only yesterday that on the banks of the Jamuna, your caravans performed

wazu? Today, you are afraid of living here. Remember, Delhi has been nurtured with your blood. Brothers, create a basic change in yourselves. Today, your fear is misplaced as your jubilation was yesterday.

The words coward and frenzy cannot be spoken in the same breath as the word Muslim. A true Muslim can be swayed neither by avarice nor apprehension. Don't get scared because a few faces have disappeared. The only reason they had herded you in a single fold was to facilitate their own flight. Today, if they have jerked their hand free from yours, what does it matter? Make sure that they have not run away with your hearts. If your hearts are still in the right place, make them the abode of God. Some thirteen hundred years ago, through an Arab *ummi*, God proclaimed, "Those who place their faith in God and are firm in their belief, no fear for them nor any sorrow." Winds blow in and blow out: tempests may gather but all this is short-lived. The period of trial is about to end. Change yourselves as if you had never been in such an abject condition.

Brothers, keep up with the changes. Don't say, "We are not ready for the change." Get ready. Stars may have plummeted but the sun is still shining. Borrow a few of its rays and sprinkle them in the dark caverns of your lives.

Brothers, I do not have a new prescription for you. I have the same old prescription that was revealed to the greatest benefactor of mankind, the prescription of the Holy Quran: "Do not fear and do not grieve. If you possess true faith, you will gain the upper hand."

The congregation is now at an end. What I had to say, I have said, briefly. Let me say once again, keep a grip on your senses. Learn to create your own surroundings, your own world. This is not a commodity that I can buy for you from the marketplace. This can be bought only from the marketplace of the heart, provided you can pay for it with the currency of good deeds.[3]

The speech was widely reported by the media and these reassuring and comforting words stirred the Muslims across the country most of them were shockingly scared as they were feeling isolated in the hostile surroundings intentionally created by the

Hindu Right. Besides Azad, Gandhi and Nehru too realised the necessity to impress upon the Muslims that they were rightful, equal citizens of independent India and the government agencies would protect their lives and properties. Gandhi, in particular, undertook a fast unto death demanding *inter alia* the protection of lives and properties of the Muslims who preferred to remain in India. Though, the Hindu Right had been hatching conspiracies to assassinate Gandhi since 1933, the pro-Muslim stand of him after independence proved to be one of the immediate causes for his assassination. Gandhi's murder by a fanatic Hindu having links with the Hindu Mahasabha and the RSS shocked the entire nation. There was retaliation against Hindu communal forces and the Home Ministry under Vallabhbhai Patel had banned the RSS. Though the ban was lifted after a year, the Hindu Right appeared to be on the defensive.

Nehru too addressed many Muslim gatherings and tried to infuse their hearts and minds with encouraging words. He got himself engaged in practically quelling the anti-Muslim riots in and around Delhi. The most concrete guarantee of security for the Muslims appeared on November 26, 1949, when the Constitution of India was adopted by the Constituent Assembly. With Nehru, B.R. Ambedkar and Azad as the leading members of the Constituent Assembly, Part III dealing with the justiciable Fundamental Rights enshrined Right to Freedom of Religion (Articles 25-28) and Education and Cultural Rights (Articles 29-30). These rights are of course guaranteed in all civilised liberal democracies but for the Muslims of India, barely two years after the creation of Pakistan, they were sanctification of the promises made to them by the prominent Congress leaders. This clinched the issue. For most Indian Muslims across the country the INC, which turned into a political party, emerged as the protector of their lives and properties. This security-engendered-phase during which almost all Muslim voted en bloc to the Congress spanned over a period from 1951-1967. It must however, be pointed out that at least in the first three general elections the voting behaviour of most Hindus was similar to that of the Muslim. The Congress dominated the electoral scene during the Nehru years and in consequence of this Myron Weiner called it a 'single-party-dominance-system'.[4] The inference that the Muslims have been voting en bloc for the Congress is equally valid for the majority community.

Additionally, there was at least a pocket in the South where the Muslims did not vote for the Congress. In the South the Muslim League got a new incarnation. Since the Southern Muslims did not suffer much with the guilt feeling because of the creation of Pakistan and the Hindu Right was not very active in the Southern States, the conditions for Muslims were not as suffocating as they were in the North. Therefore, the South Indian Muslim leaders formed the Indian Union Muslim League on March 10, 1948 in the then Madras city. In the very First General Elections, the IUML won a Lok Sabha seat in Kerala and since then it always had a presence in Parliament. Though formation of a separatist political party accentuating the religious identity of a minority community does not get along with the characteristic of a secular democracy, it proves in clear terms that the Muslims are not socially or politically a homogeneous entity.

It must be pointed out that Jammu & Kashmir (68.31%),[5] Assam (34.2%)[6] West Bengal (27%)[7], Kerala (24.7%)[8], Uttar Pradesh (19.26%)[9] and Bihar (16.87%)[10] are the states where the Muslim population is sizable and in quite a few constituencies of these states the Muslim votes significantly affect the results of the elections. In the First General elections 1951-52[11], if we take into account the election results of 489 Lok Sabha seats, the Congress won 364 seats and except one Parliamentary constituency of Kerala it could register comfortable winning margins in all the Muslim dominated constituencies. No elections were held for Parliament in Jammu & Kashmir, the only Muslim majority state but in other states where the Muslim population was sizable it was the Congress that bagged the Muslim votes. In Assam, where Muslims constituted about 35% of the total population, the Congress won 9 of the 10 seats, In West Bengal, where Muslims comprised 27% of the population, the Congress, despite the formidable challenge from the CPI, could win 10 of the 16 seats, In Uttar Pradesh where at that time the

Muslim percentage of the population was about 20%, the Congress won 80 of the 85 seats, in Bihar where the Muslim presence was around 17%, the Congress won 45 of the 55 seats.

The picture was not much different in the Second General Elections of 1957[12] as well. Again there were no elections for Parliament in Jammu & Kashmir. In Assam, the Congress won 9 out of 12 seats, in West Bengal 23 of the 33 Lok Sabha seats. After the reorganisation of Indian states, in Kerala the Muslim constituted one-fourths of the population. However, the CPI had a strong presence there capturing 9 of the 18 seats. Nonetheless, in the 6 seats the Congress won the Muslim voters played the crucial role. In West Bengal Congress could win 23 of the 33 seats, whereas in Uttar Pradesh it could win 72 of the 85 seats. In Bihar the Congress tally was 41 of the 55 seats.

In 1962[13], the last General Elections under Nehru's Premiership, once again no elections were held for Lok Sabha seats in Jammu & Kashmir. In Assam, the Congress won 9 of the 12 seats, In West Bengal 23 of 36 seats, in Kerala the Congress and the CPI could win 6 seats each, whereas the Indian Union Muslim League could win 2 of the 18 seats, in Uttar Pradesh the Congress won 62 of the 85 seats, whereas in Bihar it bagged 39 of the 55 seats.

The elections for the Fourth Lok Sabha[14] were held at a time when the nation was confronted with quite a few problems. India had to fight two major wars during the first five years of the seventh decade of the last century; first in 1962 against China and then in 1965 against Pakistan. The period also saw the death of Pandit Jawaharlal Nehru, who is rightfully, regarded as the architect of modern India. Nehru's successor, Lal Bahadur Shastri had also died in January 1966. For the Congress, therefore, it was difficult to bank upon as charismatic a leader as Nehru. Consequently, Congress had to face quite a few setbacks and the political observers, based on the results of the elections, pronounced the 'end of the Congress system'. Nonetheless, it needs to be underscored that the Muslims did not desert the Congress even in the Fourth General Elections and that is the reason to expand the first phase of the Muslim voting behaviour till 1967. In 1967, first time elections for the Parliamentary seats were held in Jammu & Kashmir and Congress won 5 of the 6 seats. Though the performance of the Congress in many states, in particular in the Hindi heartland, was far from satisfactory it could win 10 of the 14 seats in Assam. In West Bengal, however, the Left parties started flexing their muscles, yet the Congress with the loyal support of the Muslim voters could win 14 seats, the maximum any single party could manage to bag. In Kerala it was the CPM that emerged winning 9 of the 18 seats and it was presumed that in certain constituencies the Muslims shifted their loyalty from Congress to the CPM. It was for that reason the Congress could win only one seat. IUML, however, continued to hold the 2 seats it won in the previous elections. In Uttar Pradesh the Congress could win 48 seats and the Muslims continued to support Nehru's party. In Bihar too the Muslim base of the Congress remained intact as it could win 34 seats.

The elections for the fifth Lok Sabha were held a year earlier in 1971[15]because of the internal turmoil of the Congress. Indira Gandhi who was elected as the leader of the Congress and the Prime Minister over Morarji Desai did not get along well with the senior leaders of the Party who intended to keep her under their thumb. She refused to toe the line and rebelled causing a split in the grand old party. The anti-Indira faction of the Congress came to be known as the Congress (O), while the faction she led was called Congress (R). Though she had the support of most of the Congress MPs, the Congress (R), however was reduced to a minority of 228 seats in a House of 522. There was also an external factor that made Mrs. Gandhi immensely popular across the country and it was the Indo-Pak war over the issue of Bangladesh. Her handling of the refugee crisis and the ultimate courageous decision to support the Bengali rebel forces against the Pakistani army despite the clear American threat, added tremendously to her image as a strong leader. She went to get a new mandate from the people of India with the catchy slogan of '*Garibi Hatao*' (eradicate poverty) that sent a message to the people that the Congress (R), in addition to being secular and democratic was also socialist. She came back to power with a thumping majority. The result did not show Muslims voting differently than the majority community. Most Indians voted for the party led by Mrs. Gandhi and so did the Muslims.

In Jammu & Kashmir Congress (R) repeated its performance of the previous elections winning 5 of the 6 seats. In Assam it could win 13 of the 18 seats, whereas in West Bengal, the CPM could further improve its position by winning 20 of the 40 seats while Congress (R) managed to bag 13 seats. In Kerala, the Congress won 6 of the 20 seats though it emerged as the Party having won the largest number of seats. In Uttar Pradesh, Mrs. Gandhi's party swept the polls winning 73 of the 85 seats and in Bihar it bagged 39 of the 55 seats. These results of the states having a sizable Muslim population had no divergent feature that could be mentioned to show out of the ordinary Muslim electoral behaviour.

II. The Coming-of-Age Phase of Political Self-Assurance (1977-1989)

During the second phase spread over 15 years the Muslims first voted against the Congress but in the remaining elections reluctantly went back supporting it. The creation of Bangladesh had brought a positive change among the Muslims as citizens of India. First of all the chimera of Pan-Islamism got an un-ceremonial burial from the mindset of the Muslims. Secondly, those who had a soft corner for Pakistan were stirred from their deep slumber to face the unpalatable reality. The way the West Pakistani army raped, massacred and looted the Bengali Muslim women, men and their properties rudely shocked them and then they realised the futility of the religious bond. Thirdly, they realised that they had to live and die in their motherland alone and in view of this realisation they completely focused on fighting as the rightful citizens of the country. Fourthly, the vulnerability of the Congress exposed in the 1967 elections made the Muslim realise the worth of their votes which they would be using with considerable self-assurance in future elections. Therefore, they, like most Indians, voted against the Congress in 1977 but, again like most Indians embraced it in other elections.

The exceptional development during the period between the fifth Lok Sabha elections in 1971 and the sixth Parliamentary elections of 1977 was the proclamation of national emergency that continued for 19 months from June 25, 1975 to March 21, 1977. The excesses committed during this period mainly by the Youth Congress members led by Sanjay Gandhi made Mrs. Gandhi extremely unpopular that impacted the results. The duration of the fifth Lok Sabha was extended by a year during the emergency and on January 23, 1977, Mrs. Gandhi called for fresh elections. The leaders of the Congress (O), the Jan Sangh, the Bharatiya Lok Dal and the Socialist Party, many of whom had been incarcerated during the emergency, hastily formed a joint front in the form of the Janata Party under the patronage of Jayaprakash Narayan to challenge the Congress. The Janata Party turned the campaign as a fight between 'democracy and dictatorship' and convinced the masses that under Mrs. Gandhi India would no longer remain a democratic republic. The results were spectacular but not surprising. It was for the first time the Congress lost power at the Centre. The Janata Party won 298 of the 524 Lok Sabha seats and Morarji Desai became the first non-Congress Prime Minister of India. Nevertheless, the Congress could do well in the Southern states and in the Western states of Maharashtra and Gujarat the results were mixed. This was the first elections when the Muslims electorates mainly voted against the Congress but their voting behaviour was in tune with that of the majority community.

Looking at the election results[16] of the states with sizable Muslim populations, in J & K the Congress lost 2 seats as its tally was reduced to 3 from 5. In Assam too it lost 3 seats as it could win 10 instead of 13 as it did in the last elections. In West Bengal it could settle for only 3 seats as CPM (17) and Bharatiya Lok Dal, a component of the Janata Party, could win 15 seats. In Kerala the Congress actually increased its tally by 5 seats winning 11 of the 20 seats. Here the Muslims, in contravention to the voting behaviour of the Muslims of the North, supported the Congress. It was in Uttar Pradesh and Bihar that the Muslims hugely deserted the Congress along with all the other communities as in both the states the Congress could not win a single seat. Mrs. Gandhi herself lost the election from her pocket borough of Rae Bareilly.

The internal ideological contradictions of the political partners of the Janata Party were so glaring that this coalition of a party hardly had a chance to complete the five-year term in office right from the word 'go'. The popular perception was that Morarji Desai favoured the pro-Hindu policies piloted by the Jan Sangh and that alienated the other partners such as the Bharatiya Lok Dal led by Charan Singh and the members of the Socialist Party. The administration got almost paralysed because of the constant bickering that forced Morarji Desai to resign from the government on July 19, 1979. President Sanjiva Reddy invited Charan Singh to form the government. His BLD had 64 members and despite his best efforts, Singh could not drum up the support of the majority of Lok Sabha members. Consequently, after remaining in office for three weeks without facing Parliament, Charan Singh resigned. President Reddy dissolved Parliament and called for fresh elections in January 1980.

The elections for the seventh Lok Sabha in 1980[17] brought Mrs. Gandhi back with a huge majority and like most Indians, Muslims too voted the Congress (I) back to power. In this elections, therefore, the voting behaviour of the Muslims coincided with the behaviour of the other communities. Taking into account the results of the states with considerable Muslim population, in J & K, the Congress won 5 of the 6 seats and in Assam it captured 13 of the 18 seats. In West Bengal, however, the CPM maintained its supremacy winning 20 of the 40 seats with Congress settling down with 13. In Kerala Mrs. Gandhi's party could win 6 of the 19 seats while its performance in Uttar Pradesh and Bihar was much better winning 73 of 85 and 39 of 54 seats respectively.

The elections for the eighth Lok Sabha in 1984[18] were held a year earlier because of Mrs. Gandhi's assassination by her own Sikh bodyguards. Rajiv Gandhi, who did not have any inclination to be a politician, was forced by the stalwarts of the Congress (I) to step into his mother's shoes. In two states, Punjab and Assam elections could not be held in 1984. Thus the elections were held only for 514 Lok Sabha seats. The Congress, riding on the sympathy wave, got a thumping majority winning 404 seats and a year later when elections were held in Punjab and Assam it could add 10 more seats to its tally. Unlike the misguided perception that Muslim voting behaviour differs from the rest of Indians, the Muslims too in this election voted as members of all other communities.

In J & K, this time the Congress lost two seats as it could win only 3 against 5 as it was winning since 1967. In West Bengal it could win 16 as a significant section of the Muslim voters continued to support the CPM, which won 18 seats. In Kerala the performance of the Congress improved notably as it could raise its tally from 6 to 13. In Uttar Pradesh the Congress swept the polls winning 83 of the 85 seats and in Bihar too it captured 48 of the 54 seats.

III. The Strategic Voting Phase (1989-Present)

The strategic or tactical voting by the Muslim electorates referred to supporting any candidate fielded by any secular party who is in a position to defeat the BJP. Consequently, the Muslim voters may support CPM in West Bengal and the Congress in Kerala. For the Muslim voters from now onwards the choice was reduced to secular parties against the BJP.

Stung by the Bofors scandal, the Congress in the elections held in 1989[19] under Rajiv Gandhi could win 197 seats, far short of a clear majority. Nonetheless, no political party got a majority of seats in the Lok Sabha as for the first time it was a hung Parliament. Subsequently, various opposition parties formed a National Front under V.P. Singh. The irony was that the Left Front agreed to join hands with the Bharatiya Janata Party (BJP), though its members did not join the minority government and opted to support from outside. The BJP won a significant 85 seats and from then onwards the Hindu Right kept gaining politically. Rajiv Gandhi's political naivety to please Hindus and Muslims simultaneously and his decision to launch the election campaign from Ayodhya with a promise of establishing the Ram Rajya proved disastrous. It was for the first time, the Muslim voters in the North seemed to be deserting the Congress, particularly in Uttar Pradesh and Bihar.

Referring to the states with significant Muslim electorates, in J & K, the Congress won 2 of the 6, in West Bengal the Muslim voters largely backed the CPM that won 27 seats while the Congress bagged merely 4 of the 42 seats. In Kerala, the Muslim voters, partly because of an unwritten pact between the Congress and the IUML, helped the former win 14 of the 19 seats. In Uttar Pradesh, as pointed out, the Muslims drifted away from the Congress as the party won only 12, whereas the Janata Dal was successful in 54 of the 85 seats. In Bihar the Congress bagged merely 4 seats as most Muslims preferred the Janata Dal that won 32 of the 55 seats.

V.P. Singh's task to keep parties like the BJP and the Communists happy at the same time to ensure their outside support to his government was extremely difficult. The BJP seemed to be consolidating its Hindu base in the Hindi heartland as it had started an aggressive campaign for the construction of the Ram Mandir at Ayodhya. In response, V.P. Singh made an attempt to create a new constituency for himself by implementing the 'Mandal Commission Report' on August 7, 1990, with the hope that the backward class voters would rally behind him. The implementation of the Mandal Commission Report that gave 27% reservation to the OBCs in all the central government jobs and educational institutions led to widespread caste riots and self-immolations in the North. The BJP feared that it might lose political ground because of caste divisions among the Hindus. In order to counter the possibility, L.K. Advani began his *rath yatra* from Somnath on September 20, 1990 with the plan to reach Ayodhya on October 30, 1990 to construct the Ram temple there. The *yatra* could enthuse the common Hindus and also generated anti-Muslim feelings at some places that resulted in communal riots. The BJP threatened V.P. Singh that if Advani's *yatra* was stopped and he was arrested, it would withdraw its support to the government. In order to control the communal flare up in Bihar, the Chief Minister of the state, Lalu Prasad Yadav arrested Advani on October 23, 1990, as a result of which the BJP withdrew its support to the V.P. Singh government.

There was a revolt in the Janata Dal as well. Chandra Shekhar and Devi Lal left JD with 64 members to constitute a new political outfit, Samajwadi Janata Party. With V.P. Singh failing to get majority support, he resigned on November 7, 1990. The Congress under Rajiv Gandhi immediately extended its support to the Samajwadi Janata Party and as a consequence, Chandra Shekhar was sworn in as the Prime Minister on November 10, 1990. It was a short-lived government as Rajiv Gandhi withdrew the outside support to Chandra Shekhar on March 6, 1991. The 9th Lok Sabha was, therefore, dissolved and new elections were called. Chandra Shekhar, however, continued to be the caretaker Prime Minister at the request of the President.

The Parliamentary elections to the 10th Lok Sabha[20] were held in three phases, the first one on May 20, the second one on June 12 and the third one on June 15, 1991. Immediately after the first phase, Rajiv Gandhi was assassinated by an LTTE activist, which gave a slight edge to the Congress in the second and third phases. Nonetheless, no party could secure the majority but a veteran leader of the Congress, Narasimha Rao managed to seek the support of some parties to form the government. The Muslim voters continued to be wary of the Congress in Uttar Pradesh, Bihar and West Bengal as many of them voted against the Congress as well as the BJP.

In J & K no elections were held because of the rise in the insurgency in the state, whereas the Congress could win 8 of the 14 seats in Assam. In West Bengal the Muslim voters mostly backed the CPM that won 27 seats while the Congress tally was 3. In Kerala, however, the Congress won 13 seats, while the IUML continued to retain its 2 seats. In Uttar Pradesh Muslim voters largely voted for the Janata Dal that won 22 seats at the cost of the Congress that was reduced to 5 seats. The biggest gainer in the state thanks to the commotion over the Babri Masjid-Ram Janambhoomi controversy was the BJP that bagged 51 seats. In Bihar, with the Muslim backing the JD won 31 seats, whereas the Congress won only a single seat.

The most earth-shattering incident of the Narasimha Rao government was the demolition of the Babri mosque on December 6, 1992. It was a watershed for Muslim politics in the sense that the Congress in the North Indian states got completely alienated from the Muslim electorates. Even earlier the party was gradually losing Muslim support since Rajiv Gandhi's launching of the election campaign from Ayodhya and his vociferous declaration to bring about Ram Rajya in the country. The performance of the Narasimha Rao government was far from satisfactory. Besides its failure to protect the Babri mosque it was also embroiled in various scandals. There were corruption charges too.

Consequently, in the Parliamentary elections of 1996[21]the BJP emerged as the largest single party with 161 seats while the Congress managed to settle at 114. In J & K where the elections were held despite serious problems of law and order the Congress won 4 of the 6 seats, in Assam the tally was 5. In West Bengal the Muslim voters once again preferred the CPM that won 23 seats and the Congress bagged 9. In Kerala, though the Congress lost some Muslim votes it was not completely rejected by the community. It won 7 seats that helped it emerge as the largest single party. In Uttar Pradesh, the Muslim votes were wasted hugely as they could not vote either for the BJP or the Congress. The other parties that time were not in a position to provide a viable secular alternative. This helped the BJP that won 52 seats. The Samajwadi Party that was slowly emerging as the preferred choice of the Muslim voters won 16 seats. The BSP too got some Muslim votes as it could win 6 seats while the Congress tally was 5. In Bihar the Muslims mainly voted for the JD that helped it win 22 seats while BJP with the support of its Hindu base bagged 18, while the Congress was reduced to 5 seats.

Since it was a hung Parliament, the President, Shankar Dayal Sharma, invited the leader of the largest single party to form the government and proved the majority support on the floor of the Lok Sabha within two weeks. The BJP leader Atal Bihari Vajpayee was sworn in on May 15, 1996 as the new Prime Minister. The BJP tried to win support from the non-Congress party by moderating some of its most controversial policies but could not manage to convince the majority of the Lok Sabha MPs. Accordingly, after remaining in office for 13 days, Vajpayee resigned which forced the President to invite the Congress, the second largest party, to head the new government. The Congress refused to form the government but it showed the inclination to support a government headed by the Janata Dal. Thus the Chief Minister of Karnataka, H.D. Deve

Gowda was sworn in as the Prime Minister. Besides the Congress the Left Front also supported the Gowda government. Nonetheless, it was an edgy alliance as the free market proponents and the Marxists could hardly be comfortable in each other's company. When it became impossible for Gowda to simultaneously please its outside supporters such as the Congress and the Communists, he resigned. In order to avoid fresh elections, the Congress agreed to support the United Front government with a new leader. Thus, I.K. Gujral was sworn in as the Prime Minister on April 21, 1997. Gujral remained in office for 11 months including 3 months as the caretaker PM before the new elections.

As was projected in quite a few pre-poll surveys, the BJP emerged as the largest single party with an improved tally in the 12th Lok Sabha elections in 1998.[22] The Congress failed yet again to win back the support of the Muslims in UP and Bihar while in some states the regional parties showed signs of playing a crucial political role at the Centre in times to come. In J & K, for instance, the National Conference won 3 seats against Congress 1. In Assam, however, the Congress could win an impressive 10 seats. In West Bengal the Muslims voters loyally supported the CPM that bagged 24 seats, whereas the Congress got 1. In Kerala, the Congress won 8, while the CPM got 6. The IUML continued to retain its 2 seats. In Uttar Pradesh, the BJP further strengthened its Hindu base by winning 59 seats. The most votes largely went to the SP and BSP that won 19 and 4 seats respectively. In Bihar, the Rashtriya Janata Dal, the party founded by Lalu Prasad Yadav when he broke away from the JD a short while ago, emerged as the new favourite of the Muslims who could help it win 17 seats. The BJP won 19 while the Congress tally was 4.

The BJP with its pre-poll allies like the Samata Party, Shiv Sena, Akali Dal, AIADMK and Biju Janata Dal formed the National Democratic Alliance, which secured a majority with the outside support of TDP and once again Vajpayee became the PM. Among the NDA, except the Shiv Sena, the other parties had no ideological connection with the BJP. In fact almost all of them were regional parties with completely different agenda than the BJP. Thereafter, shortly after the formation of the government Jayalalitha, leader of the AIADMK withdrew her support in May 1999 and fresh elections were announced.

In the elections for the 13th Lok Sabha, in 1999 [www.elections.in/.../1999-election-results.html] NDA without the inclusion of the AIADMK won 298 seats, while the UPA led by the Congress managed to bag 136 seats. The Left front also won 43 seats. The Muslim opposition to the Congress in the North continued that once again resulted in the setback to the party led by Mrs. Sonia Gandhi. In J & K, the Congress was wiped out while the National Conference won 4 seats and the BJP bagged 2 seats from the Jammu region. In Assam, however, the Congress won over the Muslim voters and thus won 10 seats. In West Bengal too the Congress failed to win a single seat while the CPM captured 21. In Kerala, this time around the CPM and the Congress won 8 seats each. In Uttar Pradesh the BJP's tally was considerably reduced as they won only 29 seats. The Muslim votes seemed to be divided between the BSP and the SP, which won 14 and 12 seats respectively, while the Congress succeeded in 10 seats. In Bihar the BJP won 23 seats, JD (U) got 18, while Lalu Prasad's RJD, the favourite party of the Muslims was successful in 7 seats.

It was the first BJP-led government that successfully completed the five-year term at office. The NDA with its slogan of "India Shining" went to the polls for the 14th Lok Sabha in 2004.[23] Most election surveys indicated a return of the BJP government. Nonetheless the results surprised the political analysts as UPA with the Congress in the lead captured the majority of the Lok Sabha seats and Manmohan Singh was sworn in as the Prime Minister. The Muslims in the North, in particular UP and Bihar continued its boycott of the Congress but in other states where their population was 10 or less than 10 per cent they rallied behind the Congress to deny the BJP to assume power once again. In J & K the Congress won 2 seats against its tally of zero in 1999. In Assam, the Muslim voters did not desert the Congress as the party won 9 seats. In West Bengal the supremacy of the CPM and its Muslim base remained intact as it won 26 seats, while the Congress failed to secure a single seat. In Kerala too the Muslim voters rallied behind the Left Front as the CPM won 12 and the CPI 3 seats, while the Congress was wiped out. In UP it was the SP that continued to consolidate its Muslim base along with the OBCs as it won 35 of the 80 seats. In the meanwhile, the carving out of Uttaranchal out of UP reduced its number of Lok Sabha seats to 80. In Bihar the RJD continued the first choice of the Muslim voters as it won 22 seats out of 40. The creation of Jharkand out of the state of Bihar resulted in the reduction of the Parliamentary seats from 55 to 40. This voting pattern of the Muslim voters clearly indicated a strategic or tactical voting with the purpose of keeping the Hindu Right, in particular, the BJP out of power.

The results of the 15th Lok Sabha elections in 2009[24] were not much different from the previous election. The only difference was that a regional party that had been on the fringes earlier, viz. the All India Trinamool Congress ended the three decade domination of the CPM in West Bengal. The reason for the Muslim voters deserting the Left Front in large numbers was mainly the publication of the Sachar Committee Report in 2006. The Report revealed that the Muslim representation state government jobs was barely 4%, whereas it was 11% even in the purported anti-Muslim state of Gujarat. The shocking figures rattled the Bengali Muslims so much that they voted for the TMC almost en bloc. In J & K there was no significant change. The National Conference won 3 seats and the Congress 2. In Assam the foundation of the Assam United Democratic Front by Maulana Badruddin Ajmal split the Muslim votes which helped the BJP win 4 seats in the states. The AUDF could not win more than one seat but it damaged the prospects of the Congress whose tally was reduced to 7. In West Bengal as pointed out earlier, the TMC won 19 seats, the CPM 9 and the Congress 6. In Kerala, the see-saw battle between the Congress and the CPM continued as this time around the former won 13 and the latter 4 seats. In Uttar Pradesh the Muslim votes were again divided between the SP and the BSP. According to a survey conducted by the Centre for the Study of Developing Societies (CSDS), the Muslim support to the SP was significantly eroded from 75% to

30% in 2009. The reason was the SP's decision to join hands with Kalyan Singh who was BJP Chief Minister of UP when the Babri mosque was demolished. Though SP won 23 seats, it could have bagged many more had there been no shift of the Muslim voters away from it. Many Muslims voted for BSP that helped it win 20 seats. The Congress managed to get some Muslim votes that helped it succeed in 21 constituencies but quite a few Muslim voters wasted their votes. In Bihar, Lalu Prasad Yadav's image got a severe beating because of his alleged involvement in the fodder scandal and for that reason it was believed that the Muslim voters shifted their loyalty to the JD (U) that won 20 seats and the RJD 4. Here the Muslim voters shunned the Congress hugely which secured merely 2 seats.

The most curious development that emerged before the 16th Lok Sabha elections of 2014[25]was the projection of the BJP leader Narendra Modi as the sole saviour of India from 'imminent destruction'. Though he was the Prime Ministerial choice of the RSS-BJP, Modi's party affiliation was almost relegated to the background. It was Modi all the way and the catch-line for the Hindu Right was "*Ab ki Baar Modi Sarkar.*" There were serious allegations of corruption against the Manmohan Singh government which were propagated massively by the BJP and some civil society groups that were more than usually supported by the Hindu Right. For instance, Anna Hazare's anti-corruption movement and also the Baba Ramdev campaign against corruption of the UPA-2 did have the backing of the BJP and RSS. Manmohan Singh as Prime Minister hardly did anything to counter the aggressive campaigns against his government. His reticence was largely construed as admission of guilt by the people at large and ultimately the Congress had to pay a heavy price for this.

The Indian general elections of 2014 were spread over 9 phases from April 7 to May 12, 2014. It made them the longest period for the conduct of election. The NDA won 336 seats and for the first time the BJP on its own won a simple majority in the Lok Sabha by seizing 282 seats though its vote share was barely 31%, the lowest for a party to form the government at the Centre.

In J & K, the PDP won three seats at the cost of the National Conference and the BJP secured the remaining 3. In Assam Muslim votes were mostly wasted as the Congress and the AUDF could not join hands together. As a result, the Congress and the AUDF won 3 seats each and the gainer was the BJP that secured 7 seats. In West Bengal the TMC remained the first choice of the Muslim voters as it won 34 seats, while the Congress was successful only in 4 constituencies. In Kerala the Congress had the edge over CPM winning 8 seats against CPM's 5. It was in UP that the BJP swept the election winning 73 out of 80 seats. The SP won only 4 seats indicating that most Muslim votes were wasted for various reasons. The Congress tally was 2 as Sonia Gandhi and Rahul Gandhi retained their seats. Bihar was another state where the BJP won hugely, i.e. 22 seats, while the RJD got 4 and the Congress 2. Here again the Muslim voters wasted their votes by choosing various parties.

The forthcoming elections for the 17th Lok Sabha are very crucial as the Muslims because of mob lynching, beef ban, communal riots, frequent arrests of Muslim youths on trumped up charges, the unending campaign of labelling Muslims as terrorists by various Hindu groups and many instances of discrimination against the largest minority during the whole period of Modi rule, seem to be determined to dislodge the saffron party. The task, however, is apparently difficult because the BJP is not going to lose only because of non-availability of Muslim votes. As per an online survey conducted by the Times of India group "over two-thirds (83%) of the over 2 lakh respondents who took the survey saying a Modi-led NDA government was the most likely possibility after the polls."[26] In any case, the BJP never got considerable support of the Muslims in any elections yet it ruled the Centre twice. The UPA and the Mahagathbandhan have to work jointly and diligently to dislodge the NDA from power. There is a trend among the Muslim voters that they are likely to vote for a party or a coalition of parties that have a secular image and which is also in the position to defeat the BJP. It seems that the formal entry of Priyanka Gandhi in electoral politics and her forceful campaign in UP against the BJP might dilute Muslim opposition to the Congress. If it happens, the Congress may improve its position in the most populous state.

The Myths and the Reality

On the basis of this survey of the six states where the Muslim percentage of population is considerable one can respond to the myths that are deliberately perpetuated by the Hindu Right to polarise voters on religious lines. The myths and reality are explained below:

1. **The first myth** about the Muslim voters is that they constitute a vote bank in India.

   The reality is that the Muslims in India do not constitute a social monolith. They are as much divided on the lines of caste, ethnicity, language, culture and even religious beliefs as Hindus or any other religious community in India. Contrary to the popular belief, caste among Muslims is a reality and the mutual distrust and animosity between Ashraf, Ajlaf and Arzal is as intense as among the Hindu caste groups.
2. **The second myth** is that the Muslim voters vote only for the Muslim candidates or for the parties that are established exclusively for the Muslims.

   The reality is that Muslim voting behaviour is like the voting behaviour of the Hindus or any other community in India. As all Hindus do not vote for the parties that are purportedly established to protect the interests of the Hindus, the Muslims too do not support *en masse* these so-called Muslim parties. These parties such as the Indian Union Muslim League (IUML), All India Majlis-e-Ittehadul Muslimeen (AIMIM), All India United Democratic Front (AIUDF) and the Peace Party (PP) have their limited influence confined to specific pockets. Among these the oldest is the IUML but beyond the two constituencies of Kerala it could never win in any other constituency where the presence of the Muslims is sizable. AIMIM is confined to the Hyderabad-Secunderabad region. In the last Assembly elections in Maharashtra it, on the cue and covert support of anti-secular forces contested from a few constituencies in Maharashtra and won two seats. Emboldened by this, it contested from 7 Muslim-dominated Assembly constituencies in Bihar, again with the covert support of anti-secular forces, but could not win a single seat. Similarly, AIUDF, the party floated by Maulana Badruddin Ajmal in Assam has a limited influence in 2 to 3 Parliamentary constituencies. In the last Lok Sabha election it won 3 Lok Sabha seats but in other constituencies caused the split of Muslim votes that helped the BJP to win 7 seats. The PP is confined to some pockets of Uttar Pradesh. It first contested 21 of the 80 seats in the Parliamentary elections of 2009 but failed to win a single seat. In the 2012 Uttar Pradesh assembly elections, the PP fielded 208 candidates out of which only 3 could win. This shows that the Muslim voters do not necessarily vote for the candidates of a party that is supposed to be exclusively for Muslims.

3. **The third myth** is that the Muslims vote en bloc for the Congress.

   The reality is distinctly made clear in the brief survey above. The Muslims voting behaviour was consistently pro-Congress mostly in the North till the 1971 Lok Sabha elections. Nonetheless, this was the case with almost all the other communities. Though the non-Muslim voters limitedly deserted the Congress in 1967 in the Hindi heartland, the Muslims stuck to the Congress even then. The failure of the Janata Party brought back the Muslims as well as all other voters to the Congress in the 1981 Lok Sabha elections. This was repeated in 1984 as well. Nevertheless, since 1989, when Rajiv Gandhi started his election campaign from Ayodhya with the promise of a Ram temple, the Muslim voters, particularly in UP and Bihar started moving away from the Congress. The situation remains more or less similar till now. Despite most Muslim voters preferring the Congress, the community's overall support to it never exceeded 40%. In plain terms about 60% Muslim voters have been voting against the Congress.

4. **The fourth myth** is that the *maulvis* and mullahs or clerics control the Muslim voters.

   The reality is that the influence of the clerics remains very limited. Though the mullahs, in return for monetary gains, do try to influence the voting behaviour of the Muslims in favour of a particular party, the large sections of the Muslim voters usually ignore their exhortations.

5. **The fourth myth** is that the Muslim percentage of voters is always more than other communities.

   The reality is that the participation of Muslim voters is as much as any other community. This is also a myth spread widely by the Hindu Right to urge their supporters to vote in large numbers. There is no data proving that percentage-wise the Muslims vote in larger numbers than the Hindus or any other communities.

6. **The sixth myth** is that Muslims never vote for the BJP.

   The reality is that some Muslims about 8% did vote for the BJP in the last Lok Sabha elections.[27] It is true that an overwhelming majority of the Muslim voters never vote for the BJP but members of some Muslim sects who are business communities, particularly in Gujarat, have been voting for the BJP for the last two decades. It reinforces the argument that the Muslims are not socially a monolith.

Postscript

The results of the Parliamentary Elections of 2019 could have brought surprises to those who were expecting a far better performance by the Congress in a few states of the Hindi belt other than UP and a landslide for the alliance of SP-BSP in UP. However, from the point of view of Muslim electoral behaviour the results could not have been otherwise because the BJP-RSS through an aggressive campaign had succeeded in polarising Indian voters on communal lines. Initially the Opposition parties, in particular, the Congress seemed to mobilise middle class voters on issues like unemployment, deteriorating law and order situation, corruption, recession and failure of the economy. The Congress could also draw focus of the urban middle class on the tall promises that were made by Modi and his party that were never fulfilled. These core issues that relate to almost all Indians, nonetheless, could not hold up against a hyperactive onslaught with issues like national security, cultural nationalism and the threat to India's sovereignty from within and without. The attack on Indian security forces on February 14, 2019, by a suicide bomber in the Pulwama district of Jammu and Kashmir in which more than 40 Central Reserve Police Force personnel were killed, drastically altered the electoral scenario as the issue of national security towered over all other issues. Since the Jaish-e-Mohammed, a Pakistan-based Islamist militant group had taken responsibility and the attacker Adil Ahmed Dar was a Muslim youth, the mood of the overwhelming majority of the voters in the Hindi belt had undergone a perceptible change. Most voters in UP, Rajasthan, Madhya Pradesh, Haryana and Chhattisgarh believed that if Muslims had to be kept under the thumb then a strong Union Government headed by a powerful leader was necessary. The choice was obvious for all to see.

Muslim voters remained steadfast in their strategic voting behaviour with the ultimate purpose of defeating the BJP. This stratagem ended up being inadequate, as it did in the 2014 elections too, in face of out-and-out polarisation of electorates on communal lines. In constituencies where the Muslim presence is sizable the Hindutva proponents used it to their advantage for winning over the lower caste voters. The Muslims were exemplified as contenders for jobs that should rightfully go to the poorest among the lower castes. It explains BJP getting the huge support of the lower castes in UP and Bengal. In UP, Congress had its own reasons not to join the Mahagathbandhan of the SP-BSP because it was not prepared to give reciprocal concessions to the two parties in MP, Rajasthan and Chhattisgarh. Consequently, it proved a spoiler in UP damaging the prospects of the SP-BSP and its own. It could not form an alliance with the Aam Admi Party (AAP) in Delhi because it was reluctant to give any seat to AAP in the Punjab. All speculations of Muslims voting for the BJP, except Gujarat, are overstated. In UP they overwhelmingly voted for the SP-BSP and for the Congress in MP, Rajasthan and Chhattisgarh. In the South, in Kerala their choice remained the Congress against the 'godless' CPM. In Telangana the Muslims favoured, besides the All India Majlis-e-Ittehad-ul-Muslimeen (AIMIM) in Hyderabad, Congress and the Telangana Rashtriya Samiti depending on the candidates. In Aurangabad when a rebel Shiv Sena candidate filed his nomination against the sitting Shiv Sena Member of Parliament, AIMIM got the drift that its candidate could win the seat considering sizable Muslim voters in the constituency. Its perception proved correct and after a gap of nearly forty years a Muslim got elected from the Aurangabad Parliamentary constituency. Muslims, therefore, continue to stick to the strategic voting to defeat the forces of Hindutva.

References

1. www.census2011.co.in. Retrieved 2017-07-28.
2. See Moin Shakir, *Muslims in Free India*, Kalamkar Prakashan, New Delhi, 1972, wherein he quoted from the *Link* issue of November 9, 1969 and Y.B. Chaavan's statement in the Lok Sabha reported in *Times of India*, November 29, 1969. Also cited in Guha, Ramchandra, *India After Gandhi.*
3. Delhi Speeches, https://www.flickr.com/photos/mayankaustensoofi/22568972149.
4. *Party Politics in India*, Princeton University Press, 2015.
5. www.census2011.co.in › Religion
6. www.census2011.co.in › Religion
7. Ibid., West Bengal.
8. https://www.prokerala.com/kerala/religions.htm
9. www.census2011.co.in › Religion
10. www.census2011.co.in › Religion
11. www.elections.in/parliamentary-constituencies/lok-sabha-seats.htm

12. www.elections.in/.../1957-election-results.html
13. www.elections.in/.../1962-election-results.html
14. www.elections.in/.../1967-election-results.html
15. www.elections.in/.../1971-election-results.html
16. www.elections.in/.../1977-election-results.html
17. www.elections.in/.../1980-election-results.html
18. www.elections.in/.../1984-election-results.html
19. www.elections.in/.../1989-election-results.html
20. www.elections.in/.../1991-election-results.html
21. www.elections.in/.../1996-election-results.html
22. www.elections.in/.../1998-election-results.html
23. www.elections.in/.../2004-election-results.html
24. www.elections.in/.../2009-election-results.html
25. www.elections.in/.../2014-election-results.html
26. *Times of India*, February 21, 2019, p. 21.
27. Sanjay Kumar revealed the findings of a survey of the poll results conducted by the CSDS, March 30, 2014.

3

Muslim Voting Behaviour: Facts and Fallacies

Shuja Shakir

This paper discusses the myths that are associated with the Muslim community in general and its voting behaviour in particular. Muslims have long been treated as undesirably different from other communities and, on that account, are often communally profiled. There are four big myths to begin with:

1. Muslims do not believe in coexistence because they feel they have a superior religion and a culture to those of others.
2. They can multiply and procreate faster than others and hence would soon outnumber the majority community.
3. They are a monolithic society with an instrument of *fatwa* vertically hierarchising their political decision-making.
4. They thrive on the doles of appeasement thrown by the Congress Party.

Then there are minor myths as well, such as: Muslims vote en bloc, they vote only for particular parties, and they vote strategically to defeat the BJP. These myths shape the popular perception of an Indian Muslim, and with a biased media often exaggerating them, naively informed citizens become easily susceptible.

Myths propagated about a community generally produce a premeditated response from the society at large. For example, a white American travelling with a black person instinctively clutches at his wallet because of a popular belief that African-American people are genetically more prone to crimes. Closer home, a myth that Muslims exhibit an uncanny social and political behaviour breeds against their flexile ostracism that not only effectuates their segregation, but also entrenches a deep sense of social exclusion in the community psyche. The confinement of Muslims to ghettos lacking essential civic amenities, and the blatant refusal of the builders to sell or rent them accommodation in the Hindu housing societies are among its minor glimpses.

Since the academic constraints restrain this paper from exploring all the aforementioned myths, it will focus mostly on the myth about Muslim electoral behaviour. The paper reiterates Asghar Ali Engineer's (1977) rationalisation that Muslims do not show a voting behaviour necessarily distinct from others, and draws from the recent studies to substantiate it.

Muslim Discrimination: Historical Roots

Muslims face discrimination for historical reasons. They are blamed for staying in India despite dividing the country on religious grounds. Although an ordinary, poor Indian Muslim was never a part of the Pakistan movement, partition took a heavy toll on him both at psychoneurotic and economic levels. Despite an egalitarian constitution and an inclusive approach of the political leadership in newly independent India, the post-partition trauma left an ordinary Muslim in the chronic fear of being hounded out of the country. As the Muslims turned almost en masse to Congress by a way of defence against the unabated threats by the right-wing forces, Congress capitalised on their insecurities to turn them into a vote bank. Congress called it secularism; right-wing dubbed it appeasement; the question, however, is: how much did this idea of secularism or appeasement, as one may prefer to call it, benefit the Muslims in real terms?

Some scholars are of the view that publicising and promoting secularism as a tool of securing the future of Indian Muslims has actually done them more harm than good. "It has flattened their diversity, redefined their interests primarily in terms of religion and privileged the Muslim elite. It has also given right-wing Hindus a political tool to mobilise votes by using the empirically questionable rhetoric of a Muslim vote bank" (Verma and Chhibber, 2014). Caught between the conflicting political narratives reinforcing a redefinition of their identity, Muslims found themselves hard-pressed to prove the credentials of their loyalty to the nation. Results of all this have been devastating for the community. Increasing marginalisation and a shrinking share in the welfare benefits ensured that Muslims stayed on the fringes of development. Sixty years of independence notwithstanding, the Sachar Committee found them at par, and sometimes below, the Dalits in socio-economic indicators of development. Their gross underrepresentation in education, services and industry amply demonstrates why their participation in the formal economy continues to be as pathetic (see Robinson, 2007: 839-843). Not much has changed for the Muslims in terms of development since Sachar.

Political Relegation

To top it, the last few elections saw Muslims absolutely relegated in politics as well. That is not to say they were readily welcome in the political parties earlier. Thanks to their lowest '*winnability factor*', they were usually billed as rank outcasts. Political parties–from Congress to Leftists–rarely if ever dared to flaunt a Muslim candidate who was perceived to be a social liability when it came to garnering non-Muslim votes. The only difference between then and now is, in the past, Muslims would get at least some chance to contest in select minority constituencies. That no longer seems possible now that the Modi-led BJP has made Muslim political exclusion almost total. For example, in the UP assembly elections in 2017, the BJP won 320 seats without fielding a single Muslim candidate. In fact, it went on to win 62 out of 82 seats in the Muslim-dominated areas like Deoband. The results of elections proved that Muslims did not make any substantial difference to the BJP's electoral calculus. And these results tended to prove BJP was right in marginalising them.

Now, why did Muslims not matter in UP, despite being 19 per cent? Did Hindus get carried away to vote en masse for BJP's rhetoric of Uniform Civil Code, Cow Vigilantism (*gau raksha*), love jihad, and Triple Talaq? Or, like any other community, Muslims do not vote as a bloc, and have their vote split among various parties and candidates? The second possibility looks more realistic for a simple reason–Muslims, like the rest of the citizens, do not see eye to eye at their socio-economic problems. Problems of an average Muslim differ both from his intercommunity as well as intracommunity counterparts. Therefore, just as the issues that trouble him most influence the voting decisions of an ordinary Hindu, they do exactly the same in the case of an ordinary Muslim. It is no rocket science to know these issues are employment, income, inflation, and the availability of necessary civic amenities. They are seldom ethnic.

Intra-Community Differences

Much has been said about the intercommunity differences between Hindus and Muslims in terms of economic activities where Muslims badly lag behind the Hindus. But the realities of their intracommunity differences hardly ever enter the mainstream discourse. For instance, since Islam does not accept the existence of castes, it is believed there is none among Muslims. The fact is, in the cultural setting of Indian society, the notion of caste clearly extends beyond the sphere of Hinduism to encompass the other communities, including Muslims. Social stratification of Muslims into the Ashraf (the rulers) and the Arzal (the ruled) bespoke the prevalence of a caste dimension in the past.

In several parts of the country, the low caste Muslims have come forward to demand reservations in jobs and education at par with Dalits and the low caste Hindus. With constitutional provision for social justice unshackling their aspirations, the voice of backward (popularly called '*pasmanda*') Muslims has begun to reverberate. Although selective and meek, their "voices of dissent are significant in that they offer an interesting case of 'lay' perspectives on Islam that emerges from a situation of struggle against oppression" (Sikand, 2002).

Although the strobes might have recently turned on *pasmanda* Muslims, their presence was recorded long ago. For instance, the 1901 Census mentions 133 low castes amongst Muslims with some of them being so low that "no other Muhammadan would associate with them, and who are forbidden to enter the mosque or to use the public burial ground" (Fazal, 2006).

A fair-minded constitution notwithstanding, age-old cultural practices ingrained in the prejudiced mindset are not easy to remove, at least in a caste-divided country like India. There are reports that mosques in several parts of the country do not allow entry to the Bhangi (scavenger) Muslims. Several provocative evidences of the practice of untouchability against low caste Muslims in respect of inter-dining and other social interactions have also been found across several regions of UP (Trivedi et al., 2016). That vindicates Delage's argument (2014) that the "egalitarian view of Islam contrasts sharply with the functioning of Muslim society in the Indian subcontinent, whether medieval or modern, in which principles of hierarchisation and deeply unequal relations govern."

Two formidable forces–internal and external–counteract the demands of backward Muslims. Internally, the elite Muslim class opposes them because it believes classifying the community along caste lines would fracture the religious unity. Externally, while Muslim OBCs have been included in the backward category, they remain deprived of actual benefits on account of their underrepresentation in services. "As of now, the most prosperous among the backward castes have secured a disproportionate share of benefits and those at the bottom, including the majority of Muslims, have got very little" (Hassan, 2005).

Occupation and Economy: The Decisive Factor in Muslim Voting

Socio-economic status and occupational pattern are a more decisive factor in Muslim voting behaviour. Like any other society, divisions of region, class, gender and caste affect them, and it clearly reflects in their voting behaviour. For instance, the data of the UP assembly elections of 2012 showed while 26 per cent low-caste Muslims voted for BSP, only 11 per cent of their votes went to Congress, according to a CSDS-Lokniti report. A similar voting pattern was also observed in the 2009 UP assembly elections in which as against 37.3 per cent 'other' Muslims who preferred Congress, only 20 per cent OBC Muslims voted for the grand old party (Ahmed, 2014).

A sense of insecurity does underlie the general attitude of Muslims in politics, but such insecurity is a characteristic of any minority, and blowing it out of proportion does not make sense.

There is a widespread belief that Muslims record a high turnout during elections by way of a strategy to influence the electoral outcome in favour of particular parties. Reality check reveals "in the last four general elections, the turnout among Muslims was 59 per cent while the all-India figure was 60 per cent. In fact, the figures in the 2004 Lok Sabha elections suggest the turnout among Muslims was much lower than average" (Patra, 2009). Muslim turnout has actually fluctuated across the country, depending on various factors. It was held that the Muslim turnout is high in the regions where their population exceeds 30 per cent. However, this assumption is only partly supported. A study of eight constituencies with 30-45 per cent Muslim population showed rather than their larger population, it was competitive communal polarisation that caused the high Muslim turnout (Alam, 2009).

The myth of Muslims behaving like a vote bank, meaning they vote for a particular party or a candidate appears equally unfounded. The election data over years show Muslim support to political parties has never been constant (Shakir, 1990). It has varied from region to region, though the parties professing secularism have remained their first choice. The variance in the Muslim voting pattern ascertains the significance of the context in which they vote. In the post-Babri Masjid period in Mumbai, for instance, Muslims were wary of supporting the Congress for its perceived failure to protect their lives and property (Engineer, 1995). On the contrary, the data did not indicate any decline in their support to the Samajwadi Party (SP) after the Muzzafarnagar riots, although Muslims largely believed SP mishandled the riots (Pai, 2014). Contextuality is clearly palpable.

There is also a good reason to believe that the amount of influence Muslim ecclesiastics wield within the community is limited. Engineer, (1995) points out despite the Ulema Council's directives in Mumbai, Muslims did not want to support Congress after the Babri episode. In the 2004 Lok Sabha elections, the Shahi Imam of Delhi was made a part of the Vajpayee Committee and he appealed to the Muslims to vote en masse for the BJP. Not only did that happen, but even in the Chandni Chowk parliamentary constituency falling in the Jama Masjid area, the BJP candidate lost (Hashmi, 2012).

Recent Study

In order to understand who people would vote for in the 2017 UP assembly elections, Verma and Gupta (2016) did a comprehensive fieldwork survey across several districts in UP to collect the data for CSDS. Based on the facts encountered, a powerful argument that they advance against the tendency to stereotype Muslim voting behaviour is certainly worth mentioning here.

This study found that Muslims did not vote for the BJP, but the authors caution it should not be construed as a well-thought out Muslim voting strategy to defeat the party. They point out, like that of any other community, Muslim "vote choice is driven by performance, party preferences, candidates, welfare policies, and leadership among many other things." The study did not find any difference between Muslims and others on the indicators of political participation and proactiveness during the elections, based on the data of the 2012 UP assembly elections and 2014 Lok Sabha elections.

The investigators also found Muslims support was divided among several political formations in the state. The study says, in the late 1990s, approximately half of the Muslim voters in the state supported SP, which gradually came down to 27 per cent in the 2009 Lok Sabha elections, when the Muslim vote got split among the SP, BSP and Congress. Earlier, SP enjoyed more support among urban Muslims in UP. Towards 2017, this pattern reversed with more rural Muslims rallying behind the party.

Finally, the study tests a critical assumption about Muslim voting behaviour: whether Muslims coordinate with other social groups, and form local alliances to ensure the win of a non-BJP party. A multivariate analysis yielded, BJP vote share had no statistically significant relation either with fragmentation or consolidation of the Muslim vote at constituency level–so much for the myth of Muslims consolidating against the BJP.

The study concludes "while the presence of the BJP remains an important factor when Muslims make their decision about whom to vote for, that is not their sole parameter. Their choice is as much affected by issues of price rise, corruption, and employment as for any other voter" (Verma and Gupta, 2016: 115).

That is another eye-opener, among many others, regarding the misperceptions about the Muslim voting behaviour.

Postscript

Results of the recently concluded Lok Sabha elections establish two factors fairly clearly: one, that Muslim vote did not consolidate along the communal lines and two, political marginalisation of Muslims that began in 2014 continues unabated, although the number of Muslims going to the Lok Sabha showed a marginal increase from 23 in 2014 to 27 in 2019. Interestingly, all four Muslim candidates whom BJP fielded lost. The elections in 2019 constitute an extension of the 2014 elections in a sense that where BJP nurtured an unmistakable anti-Muslim image, the so-called secular parties played safe with Congress even treading a soft Hindutva line to placate the Hindu voters. Not much seems to have changed for Muslims since 2014 except the fact that the BJP emerged as a far more formidable force than what it was earlier.

The results tend to justify the contention of this paper that Muslims are not a vote bank of any political party. Going by the initial reports, the Muslim vote was fragmented between several parties. A pre-poll survey conducted by CSDS-Lokniti in March

2019 showed 26 per cent Muslims across 19 states favouring Modi. Of the 62 seats won by BJP in UP, many seats had a significant percentage of Muslim voters where BJP won by fielding non-Muslim candidates. The conclusion one can draw from these results is that either the Muslim vote got divided or it went to the BJP. Similar results came from West Bengal where in the Muslim-dominated constituency like Maldaha Uttar a non-Muslim BJP candidate defeated TMC's Muslim candidate by a huge margin. While it would be too early to ascertain the exact nature of Muslim voting behaviour in 2019 till some serious empirical studies come out, preliminary indications tend to vindicate the principal argument of this paper.

References

Ahmed, Hilal (2014), Muslims in Uttar Pradesh: Caste, Class and Electoral Politics, *Economic and Political Weekly*, Vol. 49, Issue No. 18, May 3.

Alam, Sanjeer Mohammed (2006), Whither Muslim Politics? *Economic and Political Weekly*, Vol. XLIV, No. 39, September 26.

Delage, Remy (2014), *Muslim Castes in India*, https://booksandideas.net/Muslim-Castes-in-India.html, September 29, accessed on January 11, 2019.

Engineer, Asghar Ali (1977), Do Muslims Vote as a Block? *Economic and Political Weekly*, Vol. 12, No. 11, March 12.

Engineer, Irfan (1995), Politics of Muslim Vote Bank, *Economic and Political Weekly*, Vol. 30, No. 4. January 25.

Fazal, Tanweer (2006) Dereserve These Myths, *Indian Express*, September 6.

Hashmi, Sohel (2015), Myth of Muslim Vote Bank, Kafila.org, June 15.

Hassan, Zoya (2005), Reservation for Muslims, Seminar.com (http://webcache.googleusercontent.com/search?q=cache:Fp96gjqpNuMJ:www.india-seminar.com/2005/549/549%2520zoya%2520hassan.htm&hl=en&gl=in&strip=1&vwsrc=0), accessed on January 13, 2019.

Pai, Sudha (2014), Uttar Pradesh: Competitive Communalism Once Again, *Economic and Political Weekly*, Vol. 49, No. 15.

Patra, Akshay (2009), Five Myths About Muslim Vote, *The Hindu*, April 20.

Robinson, Rowena (2007), Indian Muslims: The Varied Dimensions of Marginality, *Economic and Political Weekly*, Vol. 42, No. 10 (March 10-16).

Shakir, Moin (1990), Congress and the Minority Vote in Roy R. and S. Sissions (eds.), *Diversity and Dominance in Indian Politics*, New Delhi. Sage, Vol. II, p. 99.

Sikand, Yoginder (2002), Islamic Perspectives on Liberation and Dialogue in Contemporary India, *Economic and Political Weekly*, September 14.

Trivedi, Prashant, Goli, Srinivas, Fahimuddin and Kumar, Surinder (2016), Does Untouchability Exist Among Muslims? Evidence from Uttar Pradesh, *Economic and Political Weekly*, Vol. LI, No. 15. April 9.

Verma, Rahul and Chhibber, Pradeep (2014), Flattened by Secularism, *Indian Express*, November 05.

Verma, Rahul and Gupta, Pranav (2016), Facts and Fiction About How Muslims Vote in India–Evidence from Uttar Pradesh, *Economic and Political Weekly*, Vol. LI, No. 53, December 13.

4

Communities and Voting Behaviour: A Case Study of Jains in India[1]

Ranu Jain

Do communities have a voting behaviour? Works on voting behaviour of castes and religious communities submit that ethnic loyalties, especially religious affiliation have significant influence on the decision-making for voting. These loyalties impact directly through community and religious leadership and indirectly through family choices[2]. Choices that in common sense are considered free and independent but in Social Science literature, are seen as rational behaviour that takes into account structural constraints and feasible means towards meeting achievable goals. Families function in a socio-political milieu and are supposed to be vulnerable to manoeuvring by the community/religious leaders for gaining power or building safeguards against unwanted political controls. Are communities, whose basic unit is family, as homogeneous and influenced by community leaders or priests/ ascetics as is implied above? Social Science studies consider communities as heterogeneous and influenced by social structures like class, sect, caste, region and occupation. All these impact the voting behaviour of the community members, especially when the vote is cast by individuals in a situation where confidentiality is ensured. In such cases, the local and the personal gain significance in determining the voting choices of the individuals: individuals, whose personal requirements and exposures need not always be in line with the community. Paradoxically, in the ethnic politics of communitarian vote banks, often, the individual appears subsumed in the community especially while operating in the social networks and occupational fields historically earmarked for the community.

Myron Weiner feels that in a plural society having segmented social groups "the patterns of loyalties and interest and the power structures"[3] are often the most influencing factors for political actions. He adds, "But it will be a mistake to assume that such loyalties merely constitute sentiments...."[4] For him social loyalties have complexity "in which both sentiment and material considerations play a role ...."[5] Analysing the Nagpur votes of 1967, Kini found evidence of collective religious, caste and family voting but he considers it to be the result of "... negotiation as a campaign techniques replacing political discussion."[6] Campaigning, in general, is effective in a physical space. However, Blair discusses the limitation of the theory of physical space as an influencing factor for community voting behaviour. He states, "Some groups are geographically concentrated and have found it possible to exercise local domination through the political process....Minority groups that are geographically dispersed, however, cannot pursue such a strategy, for they have no significant areas of local control into which the collective ego may retreat."[7] Taking a position different from Blair one feels, that during a period of crisis especially when community identity and survival are challenged and when societal discrimination starts obstructing the daily life activities of the community members, collective can overtake the individual even in virtual space, building cohesion in the otherwise dispersed community. Such cohesion has a high possibility of affecting voting behaviour.

Rajni Kothari acknowledges the significance of physical space but to him the pattern of settlement is more significant than the physical space. In a settlement having a community dominance, voting behaviour may show a pattern of a community voting for a specific candidate. However, this may not be witnessed in a cosmopolitan area where competition among the candidates may be strong. He states that politics has its own social logic where it splits groups at times while cementing them at the other. To quote him, "... there is no doubt ... that castes and communities constitute effective bases for political organisation and mobilisation, the process being one of splitting or uniting social groups on political lines. Political divisions, it is found, cut across social cleavages."[8] Prevailing social factions and leadership factions aid the process of fission and fusion. For Rajni Kothari the relationship between social groups and political parties is impacted by the nature of social cohesiveness that the community enjoys. He gives instances of Muslims and Dalits as being cohesive hence having higher possibility of voting en masse compared to Sindhis. While discussing the elections in 1962, he stated:

> The difference between the Muslims and the Sindhis in the impact of politics on communal solidarity is a reflection of differences in the social assimiliation of the two communities. The sense of insecurity is much more among the Muslims than among the Sindhis who have adjusted themselves remarkably to other groups in the years since the Partition....
>
> Group collusiveness in politics diminishes further when one approaches the intermediate and upper castes among the Hindus. Here voting took place more on individual and family preferences: even families were split, the women often going against their menfolk.[9]

According to Rajni Kothari, "the influence of caste or religion seems to be critical in the case of groups which have not been assimilated into society at large and therefore lack a feeling of security."[10] Blair supports the submission. He feels that minority-majority dynamics impact voting behaviour but not always. Kini adds:

> *'Collective voting decisions tend to be taken by groups when they seek to control the rate of change and its direction'*. We offer two instances, one positive and the other negative. The negative instance is provided by Muslims who take collective voting decisions to

> support Congress. Here the occasion for collective decision is not that they are a minority community, because there are Parsis who are also a minority community but who do not take collective decisions, but to arrest the process of change that is threatening them. They are worried about a common civil code which they feel will obliterate their distinct identity as a minority community with a distinct culture. Here they can't afford to take the chance of individual rationality of decision which may mean common civil code due to division of opinion. The collective and transcendent purposes of arresting the threatened change override the operation of individual rationality....This change... cannot be achieved by individuals being left to themselves and through the play of individual rationality alone ...[11]

Although not agreeing with Kini's analysis of the voting behaviour of the Muslims and Parsis, it will be important to state that Kini's statement draws attention towards heterogeneity witnessed not only at the community level but also at the level of intention behind voting. This combined with Rajni Kothari's submission on the extent of assimilation and the level of insecurity in a community as determining factors behind voting, brings forth the need to acknowledge the impact of minority-majority dynamics on the voting behaviour of communities. Consideration of minority-majority dynamics adds the dimensions of recognition of identity, interest and rights in the discourse. Blair feels that the collective impact gets conspicuous when the minority communities "...insist on retaining their solidarity and group identity."[12]

The concept of minority cannot be taken as a homogeneous concept. For Louis Wirth[13] a minority community is essentially a disadvantaged underprivileged community, which is not allowed full participation in the public life of a nation. However, recent works have recognised that a minority community can be powerful and can have privileges. Laponce[14] differentiates between Minority by Force and Minority by Will. He feels that Minority by Force are those who have been excluded by the wider society despite their desire for assimilation. Rules, customary practices and stigma preventing political and social discrimination can result in the assimilation of these minorities in the wider society while, depending upon historical reasons Minority by Will might project and safeguard their exclusive identity and boundaries. They want to be treated as distinct cultural groups and want the rights and privileges that make the group life advantageous. A Minority by Will has a distinct culture and wants to preserve it. It may use both legal and political tools for the purpose. The first leads to rights and the second to power. A major difference, as witnessed in India, between the Minority by Will and Minority by Force is that the former as such does not face discrimination and has access to state institutions and resources while the latter not only faces discrimination but also obstructions in accessing the public resources. Examples of the two kinds of minorities can be found in the Jains and Parsis being Minority by Will and, Muslims being Minority by Force. Minority by Will are generally found to have cultural and economic resources. The voting behaviour of the two types of minorities cannot be similar. As much has been written on the voting behaviour of the Dalits and Muslims, i.e. Minority by Force, and not much literature is available on the voting behaviour of Minority by Will or that pertaining to the Jains and Parsis, the present paper looks at the voting behaviour of Jains or the Minority by Will.

Stereotypical Image of the Jains

The Jain community is a minority community but a minority that would not fit in the definition given by Louis Wirth. Jains are supposed to be affluent and powerful. Unlike the disadvantaged Minority by Force, they do not suffer from a sense of insecurity. The community is supposed to have close proximity and a high degree of assimilation with the majority community, to the extent, that sometimes some Jains even identify themselves as a Hindu caste. The community is noted for observing Hindu festivals along with its own specific ones.

The popular image of the Jains is a very homogeneous image, projecting the community as an affluent community with its members employed mainly in trading and moneylending. The community is supposed to have economic rather than political aspirations. Theoretically, based on the principle of non-violence, the Jains claim not to get involved in occupations like cultivation and menial jobs as these supposedly result in comparatively more violence (killing of bacteria and germs) than trading and money lending. Further, it is stated that the high stakes involved in trading and moneylending makes it important for the community to present a cohesive front. The checks and balances linked to multiple role sharing facilitate smooth business exchanges. Business transactions with the locals also requires for the community to be accepted as trustworthy by the locals. Such a trust generally gets built on similarity. Similar is familiar hence has higher possibility of being trusted for risky exchanges in business involving high stakes. The Jain philosophy enables a Jain to build this familiarity by allowing the community members to follow the local way of life and customs. Not being political and being conservative/family oriented, are some other features that are supposed to have helped the community in building trust with the wider society. This image of the Jain community appears to have got constructed over the image of affluent trading and moneylending Jains from Rajasthan and Gujarat. This population is claimed to be a BJP supporter.

Other than one study by V. Sangave[15], one does not come across works of a sociological nature on the Jain population. In the absence of sociological analysis, it becomes difficult to refute or support the above mentioned stereotypical image of the Jain community. However, insiders' information, interviews with Jain laities and received literature especially census data, help in capturing heterogeneity prevailing in the community. In the face of lacunae of data on the Jain community, the author conducted a quick study on the Jains in order to understand not only the heterogeneity prevailing in the community but also in its voting behaviour. The study covered around twelve respondents for intensive interviews while also getting information from kith and kin with whom the author came in contact being an insider to the community.

Almost all the respondents approached for the study observed that the occupations of trading and moneylending are mainly associated with the Jain population of West India. According to Census 2011, Rajasthan covers 14 per cent of the Jain population while 13 per cent inhabit Gujarat. However, Jains from Rajasthan and Gujarat have migrated all over India strengthening the image of Jains being mainly a trading community. For instance, in her study on the Jains of Kolkata, the author found the community as having migrated from Rajasthan.[16] Mumbai has a mixed population comprising both Svetambars and Digambars from Gujarat and Rajasthan as well as from other states of India including natives of Maharashtra.

Although acknowledging that around 83% of the Jains fall in the census category of 'other occupation' hence have a high possibility of people occupied in trading and moneylending, the Census 2011 reports Jains to be involved in other occupations also such as, cultivation (9.03%), agricultural labour (3.66%) and household industry (3.81%). Who are these Jains? An analysis of state-wise pattern shows that around 92% of the Jains reside in 8 states and union territories of India. These states are Maharashtra (31.46%), Rajasthan (13.98%), Gujarat (13.02%), Madhya Pradesh (12.74%), Karnataka (9.89%), Uttar Pradesh (4.79%), NCT of Delhi (3.73%) and Tamil Nadu (2%). Almost all these states report the majority of the domicile Jains (above 80%) as falling in the census category of 'other' occupations, which in popular image, gets interpreted as pertaining to trading and moneylending. Category of 'other' occupation is ambiguous and misleading due to its vast coverage. It includes trading as well as service sector and freelance professional activities. More specifically, a higher percentage in the category of other occupations should not be interpreted as indicative only of occupations like trading and moneylending. In fact, the percentages of Jain cultivators inhabiting the above mentioned states and union territories is worth a mention and a quick analysis. Delhi, Gujarat, Rajasthan, Tamil Nadu and Uttar Pradesh report a small percentage of cultivators (less than 4%), while the states of Karnataka (32.54%), Maharashtra (10.24%) and Madhya Pradesh (7.13%) have a significant percentage of population involved in cultivation. The share of agricultural labour in the state population of the Jains is also significant in the three states with Karnataka having 12.86% agricultural labour (AL), Maharashtra 3.17% and Madhya Pradesh 3.36%. The percentage of AL is significant in view of the fact that in other states except Tamil Nadu (3.55%) and Uttar Pradesh (3.41%), this percentage falls around or under 1%.

Most (approximately 43%) of the cultivators belong to the adjoining area of Maharashtra and Karnataka. The Jain population in this area is known as Chaturtha Jains. To quote from a non-government organization of Chaturtha Jains, Dakshin Bharat Jain Sabha also known as South Indian Jain Association, "The organization was founded in 1899. It was originally found to represent the Jains of the southern Maratha Country of the Bombay Presidency including Kolhapur State, Belgaum and Sangli.... The organisation mainly seeks to represent the interests of the native Jains of Maharashtra (Marathi Jains), Karnataka (Kannada Jains) and Goa."[17] A comparatively detailed discussion on the Chaturth Jains is available in a small e-note, "Jains–A Must Watch."[18] It states:

> Chaturths are concentrated in the southern part of Maharashta and northern part of Karnataka, mainly in Sangli, Kolhapur, Belgaum, Solapur, Hubali and Bijapur districts. Beside these districts, they are also found in western Maharashtra and central Karnataka. They are spread over several hundreds of villages in this area. In many villages of their concentration, their density is 40 to 70 per cent of the population. Generally such villages are known as 'Jain Villages'.... The traditional occupation of Chaturths is cultivation.... They are not big landowners and many families have a very small piece of land. It is due to the partition of the lands because of the growing population.
>
> The spread of education has given them more opportunities to work in other fields. So we can see many people from this community working as teachers, engineers, medicos, businessmen, lawyers, skilled workers, etc. Teaching is a popular career both among Chaturth men and women. A considerable number of people from this community also work in Police and Armed Forces.... Even women from this community have joined

> the forces. Many other Chaturth men and women are working in Maharashtra and Karnataka Police as cops and officers. In armed forces, they are generally seen in the Military, while some are in the Indian Air Force. Milking buffalos is one of the income sources for many Chaturths in villages. In their villages, they have formed cooperative milk societies, which collect milk from all over the village and send it to cities.
>
> A few Chaturth families are from the lower income group. Many families in villages have no land or have very small land. Generally men and women of this group work as labourers on other's farms or as servants in shops and small business houses.

The note also talks about the political behaviour of the Chaturth community.

> Most of the Chaturths are traditionally supporters of the Congress Party. But eventually they support other secular parties like Rastravadi Congress Party (NCP), Janata Dal and Independent candidates. As the main occupation of Chaturths is cultivation and they are born cultivators, they always support Farmer's Organizations in their causes. They rarely support Hindutva parties like the BJP and Shiv Sena....They get a considerable representation in Zilha Parishads, Taluka Panchayat Samitis, Municipal Corporations and municipalities of this region. So we can see ZP and Panchayat Samiti presidents, Mayors, ZP members and city corporations from this community.

Similar statements have been made by the respondents covered for the study. They noted that Chaturth Digambar Jains dominate interior Maharashtra and Karnataka. According to the Jain scholar Manish Modi, "They are original Jains, converts from the Nirgranthi school of thought and hence are not so close to Hindu identity. Further they, in general, are not traders but large numbers are involved in cultivation and other occupations like journalism and managing many non-government organisations. They are also not supposed to be as affluent as the Marwari/Gujarati Jain traders. These Jains like any other citizen of India, have political inclinations". Almost all the Marathi Jain respondents endorsed the statement and stated that they will not vote for the BJP or

Modi. Bal Patil who led the socio-political movement for minority status for the Jains belonged to this population of Chaturtha Jains. It is interesting to note that the call for minority status was resisted and criticised by the trading community of the Jains.[19]

Political Behaviour of the Jains

Although the quotation from the e-note, "Jains–A Must Watch" has a statement on the political behaviour of the Chathurth Jain community, one does not come across works on the political participation and electoral behaviour of the Jains. A study of this nature is difficult to undertake especially when one realises that the small size of the Jain community makes the community 'lost' in the electoral wards, in general, not significantly affecting the electoral results of the wards. Even a ward wise analysis of the election results may not help in comprehending the voting behaviour of the Jains especially because Jains and Hindus have many common surnames. In such circumstances, attempts to deduce trends in the voting behaviour of the community can be made by combining data collected from different formal and informal sources. Such inferences can be treated as postulates for further research.

Through a discussion on the Marathi Digambar Jains, the paper has problematised the popular image of the voting behaviour of the Jain community. The Chaturth Digambar Jains appear to have voting choices that negate the stereotypical image of the Jains supporting BJP. Does this help in hypothesizing that the sectarian ideologies pertaining to Jainism influence the voting behaviour of the community? Can we state that all Svetambar Jains favour the BJP or Shiv Sena political party while the Digambar Jains, whose exposures, occupational interest and personal choices reflect individual decisions, prefer otherwise? Such a submission will be difficult to make in view of the lack of sect-wise analysis of the voting behaviour of the community. In reality, due to the small size of the community, the Jain politicians rarely assert their religious identity. The assertion of the sectarian identity is even rarer. In fact, very few Jain politicians mention sect in their personal profile posted on public platforms. It is not to state that the Jain politicians do not seek community support rather that this support appears more as functioning at the immediate primary socio-political space of the politicians. Reference is being made to the kith and kin support. Underplaying of the religious identity facilitates getting support from other community members residing in the area. In such cases personality, political ideology and contemporary functional value of the candidate gain more relevance compared to their religious affiliation. The religious community decision gains importance in only those political spaces where the size of the community is significant enough to influence the electoral result of the candidates. Interestingly, even in such spaces the Jain community does not show preference for a specific political party. The case of Sagar constitutency of Madhya Pradesh illustrates the point. The landed population of the Jains of Madhya Pradesh, is supposed to follow both the Congress and the BJP. A news item on the district of Sagar, Madhya Pradesh, (November 26, 2018) reveals swings in the political choices of the community. To quote from the news item

> In the saffronised Bundelkhand region of Madhya Pradesh there is one constituency where rivals BJP and Congress have depended on the Jain community over the past more than three decades for their political fortunes: Sagar....Since 1985, only a candidate from the Jain community has emerged winner for either of the parties ....Sagar has a voting population of about 2.1 lakh of which Jain voters count for more than 50,000. Not surprisingly, both the BJP and Congress have fielded candidates from that community, ...Sitting MLA Shailendra Kumar Jain has been given a seat by the BJP for a third time while the Congress has fielded Nevi Jain, a businessman from the same community in a bid to wrest the seat....Such is the political clout of the community, political observers point out, that neither of the rival parties dare take a chance with a candidate from another community for fear of a backlash....They (Jains) act like swing votes; they decide a day or two ahead of the polling day for which party they would cast their votes. Thus the community swings the election completely in favour of either Congress or the BJP," says Dr. Anupama Kaushik, HOD, Political Science

of the Sagar University. The race to encash the community card has meant that electoral battles in Sagar are not about developmental issues or Hindutva, but about local personalities. Some point out that while matters of the business community hog the limelight, other issues faced by the region get ignored.[20]

An internet search helped to generate a list of 35 Jain politicians. The list by no means is an exhaustive one, however, helps in understanding trends in the voting behaviour of the Jains. These Jains occupy important portfolios such as Chief Ministership affiliated with many political parties. Appendix A provides a state-wise analysis of these Jain politicians. Although not providing sect-wise information, the list reveals 16 out of 35 politicians as supporting BJP; 2 Janta Party; 12 Congress; 1 Janta Dal and later Independent candidate; 1 AAP; 1 Congress later Shiv Sena; 1 DMK; and 1 support Swabhimani Paksha Party (founded the Swabhimani Party in the year 2004). Interestingly, all the non-BJP, non-Congress supporters are from states other than Gujarat and Rajasthan, hence there is a high possibility of their being non-trading Jains. The Shiv Sena supporter is from Jalgaon, Maharashtra; Swabhimani Paksha Party supporter is also from Maharashtra but from Kolhapur; DMK supporter is from Tamil Nadu and AAP supporter is from UP now residing in Delhi, whose father was a teacher. Devappa Anna Shetti A.K.A. Raju Shetti of Kolhapur, Maharashtra was associated with Shetkari Sanghatana (Farmers' Organisation) of Sharad Joshi. Due to some disputes with the latter, Raju Shetti formed a new organisation named Swabhimani Shetkari Saghtana. The DMK supporter A. Rajendran holds a position of the Chairman of the Oxford College of Engineering which is located in the village of Karai Poondi, Polur Tauk, Tiruvannamalai District, Tamil Nadu. M.P. Veerendra Kumar, earlier supporter of the Janata Dal and now an independent candidate from Kerala is a writer and a journalist. Sureshkumar Bhikamchand Jain, is an Indian politician from Jalgaon, Maharashtra, who changed his party affiliation a number of times in his political career and has been elected to the Maharashtra Vidhan Sabha for a record nine times. He was elected from Jalgaon constituency in 1980 as an Indian National Congress

(Indira) candidate, in 1985 as an Indian Congress (Socialist) candidate, in 1990 as an Indian Congress (Socialist)–Sarat Chandra Sinha candidate, in 1995 as an Indian National Congress candidate, in 1999 as a Shiv Sena candidate and in 2004, as a Nationalist Congress Party candidate. In 2009, he was elected from Jalgaon city constituency as a Shiv Sena candidate.

As per analysis of the Jain politicians, the political choices of the Jain politicians do not remain confined to the BJP or Congress, which can be considered rightist or moderately rightist parties, but can get extended to other parties also including the parties that challenge the rightist wing, i.e. the socialist and the leftist parties. Bhambhri and Verma conducted a study on the electoral behaviour of religious communities in India and conducted a survey on Johri Bazaar (Jaipur, Rajasthan), where prosperous Jains and Hindus dominate and the Muslim population lies low at 35 per cent. This survey was conducted at the time of State Assembly elections in the year 1972. Historically, Johri Bazaar had always elected Swatantra Party candidate, Maharani Gayatri Devi for the Lok Sabha seat since 1962. Even in the election of 1971, she was elected. However, Rajya Sabha elections were bagged in by the Jana Sangh party since 1957. The Congress had won only once in 1952 and CPI had never been strong there. In 1972, election was fought among Ghaffar Ali (Congress–CPI alliance), Mehtab Chand Nawalakha (a Jain standing on the ticket of the Jana Sangh) and Radhe Shyam Fatehpur (candidate of Swantrata Party or the political party of which Maharani Gayatri Devi was a member). Interestingly, defying history, Ghaffer Ali of Congress-CPI won. To quote from the paper, "When we asked the respondents why they preferred their particular candidates to the others in the field, 30 out of 66 respondents who disclosed their voting choice (i.e. 45.5 per cent) told us that they were voting for the 'party'. Another 28 (i.e. 42.4 per cent) replied that their preference was for a candidate who was meritorious and honest or one who belonged to their community."[21] The paper concludes, "It is not religion but socio-economic status that is the determining factor in political behaviour."[22] The responses to the query, "Do Jains mostly support

Modi because they are entrepreneurs?" on the website Quora.com[23] support the above submission. The responses ranges from ethical stands like, "We are inclined to betterment of all living organisms on this planet (meaning of Jainism). We don't care what brand (party) he comes from. We care for what good can he do to us and the land we live on (parenthesis in original)." Further, "Jains mostly support Modi because they hope (just like any other ethnic group or person) that he will bring growth and development to India. That's all we care about. It doesn't matter who's providing it". Again, "We have seen his vision and process of governance and even the results that Modi has provided. That is one reason we think he is better than the other two (Congress and AAP) for the moment". Pragmatism reflected in the above statement supports views of Bhambari and Verma that occupational requirements and exposures have a high possibility to influence voting behaviour of a Jain individual. The sentiment echoes in the words of Pawan Jain, a Digambar Jain from Rajasthan, working in Mumbai in the business of waste papers, "we will vote for those who will extend protection to us, protection to our culture, our religion and our business". The statement has a capacity to explain the voting behaviour of the Jains. The subsequent paper attempts to explore the nature of the Jain culture and trading occupation to comprehend the statement.

The Jain Philosophy and Culture

Jainism is considered a religion promoted by human beings. The word Jainism is derived from the concept of Jina, meaning the one who has conquered the worldly passions and exercises control over sensory impulses through his own efforts. Implications of Jina is individualism, independent decision-making and responsibility towards one's own action. Digambars (sky clad) and the Svetambars (white robed) are two major sects of Jainism.

The sacred books of Jainism are considered to be of two kinds; the Purvas (14 in number) and the Angas (11 in number). Both the sects accept the loss of the original 14 Purvas. For Svetambaras the residual memory of 14 Purvas has been recorded in the form of a 12th Anga, known as Drishtivada. Digambaras maintain that the original angas recording the teachings of the Tirthankaras (prophets) have been gradually lost and there is no way of reconstructing the original teachings of the Tirthankaras. Significantly, Jainism does not have a notion of unanimous sacred texts carrying 'God's words', which cannot be challenged and has to be accepted blindly. For Jains, religious texts are accessible and open to interpretations as per changing contexts. Debates on Jainism are common in the living rooms and laities are free to differ in their opinions. Some laities even challenge the interpretations of recognised ascetics. The accessibility of the Jain literature along with the possibility of nuanced interpretations help in avoiding rise of religious fundamentalism and dogmatic usage of Jain religious principles and symbols.

Jainism promotes the notion of individuality covering independence of thinking and action. The Jain doctrine of anekantvada (non-absolutism) which is intrinsically linked to the doctrines of syadvada (relativity) and nyasa (subjective interpretation), presents an epitome of respect for differences, coexistence and independent subjective reflections. The three doctrines taken together promote the impossibility of acquiring an absolute truth till one attains omniscience or *keval jnana* thus endorsing acceptance of relative or partial truths and subjectivity in interpretation of these truths.

One of the most influential factors behind somewhat secured acceptance of the Jains by the larger society, is that the Jains do not carry distinct physical and behavioural identity markers. The community, which is dispersed all over the world, appears to follow the dominant or the local life patterns including language and dress style. It is mainly because the Jain scriptures do not prescribe a social code of conduct for the Jain laities. Instead, the laities are advised to follow the local way of life which helps in being accepted by the local society. The process also facilitates the Jains not being projected as the threatening 'other'.[24]

It is of further interest to note that unlike the dominant Hindu religion, Jain scriptures do not prescribe any principle of social organization like caste and class divisions. One does not come across any prescribed code even for the institution of marriage, an institution which facilitates boundary fixation of an ethnic group. Ideally, spouses can be selected from any community for the Jain laities. Absence of a written social code of conduct has attributed high flexibility to the behaviour of the Jain laities. The community members have been found to follow the local code of conduct to such an extent that after the sectoral differences, regional differences appear as the most significant demarcating marker within the Jain community. One witnesses decipherable population of Gujarati Jains, Marwari Jains, Marathi Jains and South Indian Jains in Mumbai who generally live in their specific cultural pockets. The community appears to have acculturated with the local cultures to such an extent that it is often difficult to differentiate among them even through their names. For instance, the last name of Shah is used by both Gujarati Jains as well as the Hindus. Yet another pertinent example can be given of the Hindu caste system. Even though the egalitarian religion of Jainism is considered a rebellion against the caste system, the community has acquired a caste like position in the middle rung of the Hindu caste hierarchy. The community members seem happy with their high caste status except for oscillation between castes like Kshatriya and Vaishya. This is especially seen in the inter-religious marriages, which are not so rare among the Jains. The community appears comfortable with marriages with Hindu Vaishya and higher castes however, is somewhat reluctant towards marriages with lower castes. Again, just like Hindus, the Jains appear to interact with the Muslims and Christians with reluctance. Consequently, though the absence of social code of conduct gives the community a scope to interact with their immediate local society without rigidity and toxic fundamentalism, it also allows for the seeping in of local structures like class, caste, communalism in the community organization and culture.

The ethnic politics prevailing in the present India, appears to have impacted the Jain population. In the year 2014, Jains have been attributed a status of minority or a status that dwells on identity projection. Identity that gets manifested in decipherable physical as well as cultural terms and gets shaped through the process of othering. The process of othering by specifying the group boundaries, identification with the group members and strengthening of the feeling of belonging accentuates the identity of a minority community. For instance, in the month of August 2015, as a reaction to a High Court case, the Jains asserted their right of the religious practice of Santhara or fasting unto death. In this context, it is pertinent to draw attention to the meat banning incident that took place in Mira Road, Mumbai. Mira Road had a practice to ban meat eating during the Jain festival Paryushan. In the month of September 2015, the practice was challenged by the Shiv Sena. Reacting to the challenge the Jain ascetic Nityanand called for voting for the BJP. This resulted in the winning of BJP in the Mira Road–Bhayander constituency. To quote Ravikant Shinde:

> If Sena and BJP are united by Hindutva, they are separated by their food culture. In order to woo Jains, a sizable constituency in the area, the BJP supported banning the sale of meat during Paryushan, the most important Jain festival. Jains, along with the vegetarian Gujarati and Marwari population, form the bulk of BJP's vote base in Mumbai and other parts of the state. A Jain *muni* too issued a video appeal to vote for BJP 'if they want to avoid seeing mutton and omelette shops at each nook and corner'. This infuriated the Shiv Sena, which equated the *muni* to a terrorist as the Sena's vote base mainly consists of non-vegetarian Marathi-speaking population. Reports of Gujarati-dominated building societies, most of whom are BJP supporters, denying permission to non-vegetarian families to buy or rent have been in the news for long, and Sena has been opposing this practice tooth and nail. During the elections, the Sena tried to remind the Jain and Gujarati population of Mira-Bhayandar how it had 'saved' them during the 1992-93 riots. But the appeal fell on deaf ears as the BJP got a landslide victory in the elections. The Sena blamed non-Marathi Hindus for its defeat[25].

Protests were non-violent but suggest political power that the community holds on the basis of its culture and philosophy.

Vegetarianism and non- violence are the two core values that the Jains hold, which also help them towards boundary maintenance. The two values bring Jains closer to the Hindu community. The incident also warns about the possible fragmenting of the process of acculturation with the majority community that the Jains experienced in the past.

Conclusion

Community behaviour influences voting behaviour of the community members but not in case of all communities and in all circumstances. As stated by Blair for taking a communitarian political stand on voting, physical proximity is important. The dispersed community members may take a consensual stand on voting in case of a crisis especially when the community leaders are effective in their campaign to bring the members together. Historical experience of the community and its socio-political status gain significance in this context. Muslims as a Minority by Force face discrimination, exclusion and a general sense of insecurity. Hence, are more vulnerable to manoeuvring by the political/community/ religious leaders. The hate ecology strengthening violence and exclusion of the community members make the members reach out to the community platforms for their survival and for smooth conducting of their day-to day life activities. In such circumstances, it becomes difficult for the community members to practise individual choice at the time of voting. They prefer to stand together and vote in accordance to the community dictates, even when the choice may reflect sectarian and spatial differences. One feels that the political dictates do not get practised on a community but on social groups.

The socio-political circumstances of the Jains as a Minority by Will are different from that of the Muslims. Jainism promotes individualism as well as acceptance of differences. It is supposed to be a community of economic, human and cultural capital, having a sense of security which does not necessitate engineering to present a cohesive front. The community members appear confident and though, at times, using community resources, are found to be asserting for public/state resources and opportunities. In such circumstances, is it possible to control the voting behaviour of the Jain community? The distance between the Digambar Jains of Karnataka and Maharashtra and, Svetambar Jains of Gujarat and Rajasthan has already been discussed along with the differences in their political choices.

Although not having an umbrella political leadership, the Jain community, by no means, can be taken as an apolitical community. As stated earlier, some of its members have been witnessed to have political ambitions but the small size of the community, except in case of some localities like Sagar (Madhya Pradesh), does not permit them to actualise their political ambition on a communitarian base, rather the Jain politicians are forced to underplay their minority/communitarian identity for acceptance and operation in the larger collectives thus, operating as an individual citizen of the nation rather than a member of the Jain minority community. The Jain philosophy promoting individualism, relativism and non-absolutism helps towards this end. The most important contribution emerges from the philosophical dictate of following local codes of conduct. Following local festivals and way of life facilitates acceptance by the larger society. Such an acceptance is necessary for success in politics.

The communitarian voting behaviour of the Jains reflects impact of the nature of the occupation of the Jain laities. The occupation of trading and moneylending requires community support, which ensures efforts towards building community cohesion.[26] Nevertheless, one cannot be sure that this cohesion engineers voting behaviour. A more feasible explanation lies in the Jains of north west India having a pro-market inclination hence, preferring a party that would facilitate their business. Pawan Jain stated that he would vote for a party that would "protect my business". BJP is seen as a party of *Banias* (Businessmen) having a business sense and hence is favoured over other political parties by the Jains. However, one is surprised at the continued choice of BJP. Although the initial image of the political party was that of supporting the bania culture. Lately the party appears to support industrialists rather than traders. Its policies of demonetisation and

GST are irritants to the small and middle class businessmen. Still, the trader banias continue to support the party. This might be due to the fact that the acute corruption witnessed in the Congress party made trading difficult for the Marwaris/Gujaratis and also because Congress was seen as a political party supporting socialism and minority appeasement. Socialism as a policy does not gel well with the capitalist inclination of the community and the supposed minority appeasement was an alienating factor as the *Bania*, who work closely with the Hindus have inculcated the 'Othering' process of the Hindus, locating the Muslims and the Christians in the category. Occupation appears to be the strongest deciding factor for voting. The Chathurth Jains who are not in the occupation of trading and moneylending appeared to have made political choices different from their counterparts from Rajasthan and Gujarat. They prefer political parties other than right wing parties. At times, the choice includes even the socialist and the leftist political parties of India.

The above discussion does not mean that Jain philosophy, culture and communitarian feelings are absolutely non-relevant. Interestingly, despite a strong prevalence of individualism and almost no mechanism for boundary maintenance, the Jains still hold together. The consciousness of being a community is paramount among the majority of the Jains. This consciousness appears to be rooted in the pride on the status of the community members and community resources but above all, in the Jain culture and philosophy, which does not bind yet is supportive as and when required by its individual members. For local collective groups, the philosophical tenets of *ahimsa* (non-violence) and vegetarianism appear the most important cultural markers that can be used for collective manoeuvring as seen in the earlier mentioned case of the Mira Road–Bhayandar constituency of Mumbai.

Succinctly, the paper submits that communities as such do not and cannot have a voting behaviour. When in physical proximity or in time of crisis the insecurity among the members may make them vulnerable towards a collective voting behaviour. A fractured history, experience of exclusion or desire for power may strengthen such an orientation. In normal political social space, an individual citizen would make his/her own decision on the basis of occupation and ideological commitment. However, the community culture under attack of any nature can bring the dispersed community population together and can result in a communitarian voting behaviour.

Postscript

The paper submitted that voting, whether at the level of individual or collectivity, is a rational behaviour. Ethnic loyalties do impact voting behaviour but not in case of all ethnic communities. Physical proximity is an important factor behind collective voting but more important is strategic campaigning to bring the community members together motivating them to vote for a political party. Such a manoeuvring necessitates effective centralised political leadership but more a requirement in the part of the community to come together. Requirements of this nature may be based on a sense of insecurity, tremendous identification with the community or political economic benefis behind working toghther for sustemance or social change. Such requirements are specific to a social situation and are influenced by local dynamics. Hence, collective voting is not a reality of ethnic or social communities but of social groups in which members are in closer proximity with each other and group leadership more assertive and accessible to the group members. However, ethnicity goes beyond local when the process of 'othering' engulfs almost all sections of the community population. The paper did discuss the fact that during a period of crisis especially when community identity and survival are challenged and when societal discrimination starts obstructing the daily life activities of the community members, collective can overtake the individual, building cohesion in the otherwise dispersed community. Evidence can be seen in the voting behavior of the Muslims in India. Muslims in the current elections mainly due to their extreme insecurity and feeling of exclusion, have voted against the BJP. Just like the elections of 2014, only 8 per cent of Muslim votes went in favour of the BJP.

Any analysis on the voting behaviour of the Jain community is difficult to make in view of the small number of the Jains. As stated the Jains, especially the traders, moneylenders and the land owners are highly acculturated with the Hindu community and share the notion of 'self' and the 'other' with the Hindus. Their small number compels them to work with the Hindus. However one sees an occupational affiliation in their voting behaviour. Although not having specific data on the election behaviour of the Jains, the result of the areas in which the traders and moneylenders dominate reflect that the trader moneylenders and the land owner Jains have voted for the BJP while the others might not have done so as is evident in the vocal/assertive participation of such Jains in the brainstorming seminars on what has caused the current election results.

Appendix A

List of Jain Politicians in India drawn from various internet websites

Sr. No.	Name	Social and Political Position	Political Party	State Affiliation
1.	Ajit Prasad Jain (1902-1977)	Union Minister for Food and Agriculture (December 1954-August 1959)	Congress	Uttar Pradesh (Saharanpur)
2.	Mishrilal Gangwal (1902-1981)	Chief Minister, Madhya Pradesh (1952-1955)	Congress	Madhya Pradesh (Indore)
3.	Dhulappa Bhaurao Navale (1910-1988)	President, Sangli district Congress (1955)	Congress	Maharashtra (Ankalhop)
4.	Mohan Lal Sukhadia (1916-1982)	Chief Minister, Rajasthan (1954-1971)	Congress	Rajasthan (Udaipur)
5.	Virdi Chand Jain (1920-2010)	Member, Lok Sabha (1980-1984 and 1984-1989)	Congress	Rajasthan (Barmer)
6.	Sunder Singh Bhandari (1921-2005)	Governor of Gujarat (1999-2003)	BJP Founder of Jan Sangh, 1951	Rajasthan (Udaipur)
7.	Nirmal Chandra Jain (1924-2003)	Governor, Rajasthan (2003-2003)	Janata Party	Madhya Pradesh (Jabalpur)
8.	Sunder Lal Patwa (1924-	Chief Minister, Madhya Pradesh (1990-1992)	BJP	Madhya Pradesh (Mandsaur)
9.	Virendra Kumar Sakhlecha (1930-1999)	Chief Minister, Madhya Pradesh (1978-1980)	BJP	Madhya Pradesh (Mandsaur)

10.	Laxmi Mall Singhvi (1931-2007)	Independent candidate-Joined BJP in 1997	BJP	Rajasthan (Jodhpur)
11.	M.P. Veerendra Kumar (1936-	Member, Lok Sabha 2017	Janata Dal (United) till 2017 Independent candidate March 2018 onwards	Kerala (Wayanada)
12.	Jayawanti N. Mehta (1938-	Union Minister of Power (1999)	BJP	Maharashtra (Aurangabad)
13.	Mitha Lal Jain (1940-	MP, Lok Sabha (1998)	Congress	Rajasthan (Pali)
14.	Kailash Bhansali (1942-	MLA, Rajasthan (2008)	Janata Party	Rajasthan (Jodhpur)
15.	Meghraj Jain (1943-	MLA (2014-2018)	BJP	Madhya Pradesh (Sitamau)
16.	Gulab Chand Kataria (1944-	Home Minister, Rajasthan (2014-2018)	BJP	Rajasthan (Udaipur)
17.	Ishwarlal Jain (1946-	MLA	Congress	Maharashtra (Jalgaon)
18.	Vijay J. Darda (1950-	Member, Rajya Sabha (1998	Congress	Maharashtra (Nagpur)
19.	Paras Chandra Jain (1950-	Member, Rajya Sabha	BJP	Madhya Pradesh (Ujjain)
20.	Tarachand Chedda (1951-	MLA, Gujarat (2012-2017)	BJP	Gujarat (Mandvi)
21.	Dilipkumar Mansukhlala Gandhi (1951-	MLA (1999 and 2003)	BJP	Maharashtra (Pune)
22.	V. Dhananjaya Kumar (1951-	Union Minister of State for Textiles (2000-2003)	BJP	Karnataka (Venur)

23.	Satyapal Jain (1952-	MP (1996 and 1998)	BJP	Punjab Chandigarh
24.	Rajendra Darda (1952-	State Minister for Energy, Finance & Planning and Minister for Industries, Maharashtra (2009)	Congress	Maharashtra Yavatmal
25.	Mewaram Jain (1953-	MLA	Congress	Rajasthan (Barmer)
26.	Vijay Ramniklal Rupani (1956-	Chief Minister, Gujarat (2016-present)	BJP	Gujarat (Rajakot)
27.	Pusp Jain (1956-	MLA (1999 and 2004)	BJP	Rajasthan (Pali)
28.	Devappa Anna Shetti, A.K.A. Raju Shetti (1967-	MLA (2009 and 2014)	Swabhimani Paksha Party, founder, 2004	Maharashtra (Kolhapur)
29.	A. Rajendran	MLA (1989 and 1996)	DMK	Tamil Nadu (Polur)
30.	Pradeep Jain Aditya (1962-	MP (2009)	Congress	Uttar Pradesh (Jhansi)
31.	Sureshkumar Bhikamchand Jain	MLA (Nine times since 1980)	Congress Shiv Sena (Changed party affiliation many times)	Maharashtra (Jalgaon)
32.	Anil Jain	Member, Rajya Sabha (2018-)	BJP	Uttar Pradesh (Ferozabad)
33.	Satyendra Kumar Jain (1964-	Cabinet Minister (2013-2014)	AAP	Delhi
34.	Kavita Jain (1972-	MLA	BJP	Haryana (Sonipat)
35.	Abhayachandra Jain	MLA (2013-2018)	Congress	Karnataka

References

1. This paper has been presented in a conference on "Communities as Vote Banks: Electoral Behaviour of Indian Voters". The author thanks participants for sharing their views on the paper. Special thanks to Prof. Zaheer Ali without whose support the paper would not have seen the light of day. Thanks are also due to Ms. Anchal Jain for her support in collecting data for the paper.
2. See (i) Kini, N.G.S., 1974, *The City Voter in India: A Study of the 1967 General Elections in Nagpur,* Abhinav Publications, New Delhi and (ii) Sachidananda, 1976, *The Tribal Voter in Bihar*, National Publishing House, New Delhi.
3. Weiner, M. and Kothari, R. (eds.), 1965, *Indian Voting Behaviour,* Firma K.L. Mukhopadhyay, Calcutta.
4. Ibid., p. 7.
5. Ibid., p. 8.
6. Kini, N.G.S., 1974, *The City Voter in India: A Study of 1967 General Elections in Nagpur*, Abhinav Publications, New Delhi, p. 295
7. Blair, H.W., 1979, *Voting, Caste, Community Society: Explorations in Aggregate Data Analysis in India and Bangladesh,* Young Asia Publications, New Delhi-Stockholm, pp. 23-24.
8. Kothari, Rajni and Sheth, Tarun, 1962, "Extent and Limits of Community Voting: The Case of Baroda East," *Economic and Political Weekly*, September 15, 196, p. 1481.
9. Ibid., p. 1479.
10. As cited in Sachidananda 1976, *The Tribal Voter in Bihar*, National Publishing House, New Delhi, p. 113.
11. Kini, N.G.S., 1974, *The City Voter in India: A Study of 1967 General Elections in 11. Nagpur*, Abhinav Publications, New Delhi, pp. 296-97; italics in original.
12. Blair, H.W., 1979, *Voting, Caste, Community Society: Explorations in Aggregate Data Analysis in India and Bangladesh,* Young Asia Publications, New Delhi-Stockholm, p. 23.
13. Louis, Wirth, (1947(1945)), "The Problem of Minority Groups" in Linton, R., (ed.), *The Science of Man in the World Crisis*, Columbia University Press, New York.

14. Laponce, J.A., 1960, *The Protection of Minorities*, University of California Press, Berkeley.
15. Sangave, V.A., 1980 (1959), *Jaina Community: A Social Survey*, Popular Prakashan, Bombay.
16. See (i) Jain, R., 1991, *Ethnicity in Plural Societies: With Special Reference to the Jain Oswals in Calcutta*. PhD Dissertation, University of Calcutta, Kolkata (unpublished dissertation) and (ii) Jain R., 1987, "Jain-Oswals of Calcutta as an Ethnic Group–A Socio-Historical Perspective" *Man in India* 67 (4), December.
17. https://en.wikipedia.org/wiki/Dakshin_Bharat_Jain_Sabha; downloaded on March 24, 2019.
18. http://allaboutjains.blogspot.in/2011/12/origin-and-culture-of-chaturth-jains.html; downloaded on November 27, 2013.
19. See *Outlook* magazine, February 10, 2014.
20. Chakraborty, S., 2018, "In MP's Sagar, Jain comunity decides political fortunes of BJP, Congress" in *The Economic Times* (ET online), Madhya Pradesh, November 6.
21. Bhambhri, C.P. and Verma, P.S., 1974, "Voting Behaviour: A Comparative Study of the Majority and Minority Communities," *The Indian Journal of Political Science*, 35 (4), p. 338.
22. Ibid., p. 339.
23. https://www.quora.com/Do-Jains-mostly-support-Modi-be-because-they-are-entrepreneurs, downloaded on May 15, 2019.
24. For details on Jains see Jain, R. and Jain, A., 2016, "Jainism: A Philosophy Promoting Individualism, Relativity and Co-Existence" (With Anchal Jain), in Ali, Z.S. (ed.), *The Legacy of India: Pluralism, Tolerance and Peaceful-Coexistence–Religions in Dialogue*, The Wisdom Foundation, Mumbai.
25. Shinde, Ravikant, Why Shiv Sena Can't Trump BJP Using the 'Hindutva' Card', *The Wire.* January 24, 2018.
26. Timberg, T.A., 1978, *The Marwaris: From Traders to Industrialists*, Vikas Publishing House Pvt. Ltd., New Delhi.

Caste

5

The Dictatorship of the Past: Caste and the Problem of the Traumatic Excess

Murzban Jal

> The thesis of Benjamin belongs to the mainstream tradition in which prevalent idea of language and the symbolic order is that of the medium of reconciliation and mediation, of peaceful coexistence, as opposed to a violent medium of immediate and raw confrontation. In language, instead of exerting direct violence on each other, we are meant to debate, to exchange words, and such an exchange, even when it is aggressive, presupposes a minimum recognition of the other. The entry into language and the renunciation of violence are often understood as two aspects of one and the same gesture.
>
> Slavoj Žižek, 'Language, Violence and Non-violence'.

Introduction: Law and Caste or Law of Caste?

This chapter is on the language of caste and the caste of language. It claims that crisis in the public sphere is because social democracy could not be realised in India for a realisation of the full blooming of democracy. While bringing in my earlier themes of locating caste in the Indic variation of the Asiatic mode of production and the capitalism emerging thereon, as well as registering caste as neurosis-psychosis, this chapter reflects on the need for creating a new language that transcends the old language of caste and class. It concludes that the dialectical materialist transcendence of caste is of great necessity, a transcendence that will bring in confrontation with the old order of things. It claims that the functionalist mechanisms of managing caste in the form of reservation of social groups and other alleged social justice programmes are passé and that a new paradigm of operation is necessary. This search for a new paradigm is primary to understand social formations in India with special reference to caste, community and class. While debunking the Indian left's inability to interrogate caste and simply locating it as some of pre-capitalist remnant–basically in some sort of "Indian feudalism" the myth created by R.S. Sharma–it recalls Marx's nuanced reading of non-European histories. It thus not only talks of Marx's 'The British Rule in India' where caste is said to be the "solid foundation" of oriental despotism, but it also brings in Marx's unknown *Ethnological Notebooks* into the centre of scientific reasoning.

This chapter locates caste as dialectical essence (*Wesen*, as in Hegel's *Science of Logic*) from which the tree of Indian society and politics has grown. Caste as essence does not imply an essentialising process. Instead caste as essence is understood as dialectical essence, essence in a flux, yet an essence that is caught in its reified cage of unreason.

Mapping any alternative, an alternative that will give rise to the transcendence of this reified essence is what the need of the hour is. The chapter also states that behind Constitutional Democracy lies this awful essence of the iron cage of caste which in fact controls this very same democracy. But it also states that the inherent part of law is repression and that law has to be enforcement of the legal penalties that were codified and enforced earlier? Then is the Constitution of India nothing but a return of the repressed in different attire? After all one knows that in 1947 differentiated from morality (as Kant and later Althusser had so famously suggested).[1] Consider Althusser:

> Law is necessarily repressive. Kant sees and states this very clearly in his *Metaphysics of Morals* (a work that has very little of the

> metaphysical about it, its title notwithstanding). In this regard, the Hegelian conception of Law, with its delirious idealism, trails far behind Kant's.
>
> Law is repressive in that it could not exist in the absence of a corresponding system of sanctions. In other words, there can be no civil code without a penal code, which is the realisation of the former at the level of law itself.[2]

But if law as law is inherently repressive, what can one say about modern civil law and its relation to the caste system? Is the modern Indian legal system another form of an Ambedkar write his *States and Minorities* which is a revolutionary socialist document, but three years later nothing of this socialism appears even at appearance level in the Constitution of India? Why is this so?

In India there are many battles, but the battle which seems to lie in its very heart is the caste battle. Classes, political economy, the state, culture and hegemony all fall in the terrible ambit of caste and its discontents. The modern state post-1947 would become a modern caste-based state. After all, one must note that the state that emerged from the cranium of colonialism was basically a Patron State which treated citizens not as people, but as clients in economic, social, political and cultural dependence to this Patron State. The problem that all shades of the political spectrum–from the left to the right–have not critiqued this Patron State which is the main coordinator of managing the people of India basically as caste subjects.

While the Constitution of India talks of the "people of India having solemnly resolved to constitute India into a sovereign socialist secular democratic republic and to secure to all its citizens justice, social, economic and political; liberty of thought, expression, belief, faith and worship; equality of status and of opportunity; and to promote among them all fraternity assuring the dignity of the individual and the unity and integrity of the nation" where caste and other archaic institutions would wither away, the other of this very same Constitution–namely caste as the Big Other–works directly against this pledge.

It was thought that with the rise of capitalism and modernity, caste would start withering away. Instead we have witnessed new ways of caste remaking itself. While capitalism was responsible for this remaking of caste, it has been liberal democracy that is perpetually creating and recreating caste and literally shaping the language of caste. This paper claims that liberal democracy with its mechanisms of state and parliamentary elections would repeatedly recreate caste. To counter this, one needs to actively confront liberal democracy.

Here it must be noted that Nehru which not only the liberal, but which also now the left swears by, glorified caste as some sort of romantic trade union. His 1942-46 *Discovery of India* and 1936 *Autobiography*, like Gandhi's 1920 essay 'The Caste System' celebrated caste as some sort of romantic counterpart to Western capitalism. Indirect contrast was Ambedkar's 'Castes in India' which classified caste as not only an "enclosed class", but laid the genealogy of its oppressive character.

The Cunning of Reason

The multiple reservations offered to social groups largely from dominant caste backgrounds makes us remind one of Lenin's sarcastic laughter when in 1908 Maxim Gorky in the aftermath of the failed revolution of 1905 asked him to discuss philosophy. Gorky, as all know, was a part of the group called the "God-seekers" (of which the Bolshevik Lunacharsky was an important part) who wanted to discuss philosophy, mainly the new "in-thing" that "matter has disappeared". We know from Lenin's *Materialism and Empiro-criticism* that philosophy should only be understood as a lost path in fact the "falsest of false paths" (*Holzweg der Holzwege*)[3]. This is because philosophers as philosophers had become merchants for peddling bourgeois thoughts.

We know from *The German Ideology* that the philosopher "does not become a man of the world, but a bankrupt philosopher without thoughts."[4] While in Germany in the 19th century it was philosophy as speculative philosophy that ruled the roost, in India it is not philosophy as speculation, but speculation as speculation that rules the roost. The speculators are not only found in government departments eager to solve the myriad problems of

India, the speculators are found in all political parties including the communist parties and other parties that swear by the name of Ambedkar.

Creating a New Language for the Social Sciences

The term "last resort" derived from the vocabulary of the late Engels could quite possibly be the best term to explain what is wrong (in the last resort) in both theorisation of Indian social formations with specific relation to what "communities", "caste" and "class" means, as well as with democratic politics. Thus, what is wrong (in the last resort) is that the language of the social sciences and democratic politics is borrowed language. Now what is this "borrowed language" and what is wrong with it?

In *The Eighteenth Brumaire of Louis Bonaparte* Marx says that borrowed language is inauthentic and false such that "circumstances directly encountered, given and encountered by the past" functions like "the tradition of all the dead generations (that) weighs like a nightmare on the brain of the living."[5] This nightmare-like traumatic weight "anxiously conjure(s) up the spirits of the past to their service and borrows from them names, ballet cries and costumes in order to present the new scene of world history in this time-honoured disguise and borrowed language."[6]

What we are meaning is that the language used in the social sciences and democratic politics is not authentic, but borrowed from the cranium of both the upper caste elites and the colonial administration that created concepts in order to rule India. While the concepts of "Hindu" and "Muslim" were the dominant categories created by the colonial state apparatus concepts like "communities", "caste" and "class" would inevitably and unwittingly fall under the ideological cranium of this borrowed language.

One must begin with a confession that the ideas of "communities", "caste" and "class" are of great importance and debated extensively. One refers primarily to Ferdinand Tonnies's *Community and Society* and the consequent need to theorise scientifically. One also refers to Marx's essay 'The British Rule in India' where he talks of caste as the "solid foundation of Oriental despotism" and the further theorisation of caste-clan social formation in the non-European world in his *Grundrisse*, *Capital* and the last read *Ethnological Notebooks*. One also refers to his 1877 letter to the Russian Narodniki journal asking them not to transplant the historiography of the rise of capitalism in Western Europe onto the entire world and his 1882 letter to the then Narodniki Vera Zasulich that capitalism is not inevitable in the whole world and that pre-capitalist societies are much more complex than attempting them to cover then under one homogeneous system called "feudalism". For India, there was no feudalism. It is this *absence*, this *great existentialist lack* that helped the creation of the problematic of borrowed language. Borrowed language becomes not merely an ideology, but to borrow a term of Louis Althusser an "Ideological State Apparatus". And it is through this borrowed language now metamorphosed as ideology whereby people have become captives to the political machinery of the elites. And that ideology is necessarily false consciousness must be emphasised.

This chapter is on the conceptualisation of the reification of people into vote machines. What Deleuze and Guattari had called "desiring machines" we call "vote machines". The idea of language that Žižek takes up–basically from Heidegger and Lacan–from the idea of "language as the house of being" to Lacan's understanding of language as the "torture-house".[7] Žižek quotes Lacan:

> In the light of the Freudian experience, man is a subject caught in and tortured in language.[8]

He goes further:

> Not only does man dwell in the "prison house of language" (the title of Fredric Jameson's early book on structuralism), he dwells in a torture house of language....[9]

There are storms and stresses in the ideas of language: one that it is value-neutral; the second is that it is a Platonic form of goodness, and the last is that it is a prison house. This essay takes all three aspects and claims that because the language of politics is hegemonised and colonised, it serves only as a prison house. Here we must also recall Freud's 1919 seminal essay 'The Uncanny' where

Freud shows that the difference between the terms *Heimlich* (feeling at home) and *unheimlich* (literally "unhomely", though Freud talks of the feeling of dread and terror).[10]

To contextualise the idea of searching for a new language let us reflect on the quote (right at the beginning of this chapter) from Žižek who relates to Walter Benjamin's treatise on violence in his celebrated essay 'Critique of Violence'. Žižek counter-poses this Benjaminean thesis with the radical opposite one. It is not the first thesis (the humanist one proposed by Benjamin), but it's direct opposite one which states that "humans exceed animals in their capacity for violence precisely they *speak*"[11] that is more prominent and relevant today. In the age of late imperialism in permanent crisis. Thus:

> When we perceive something as an act of violence, we measure it by a presupposed standard of what the "normal" non-violent situation is–and the highest form of violence is the imposition of this standard with reference to which some events appear as "violent." This is why language itself, the very medium of non-violence, of mutual recognition, involves unconditional violence. So, perhaps, the fact that *reason (ratio)* and *race* have the same root tells us something: language, not primitive egotistic interests, is the first and greatest divider, it is because of language that we and our neighbours (can) "live in different worlds" even when we live on the same street. What this means is that verbal violence is not a secondary distortion, but the ultimate resort of every specifically human violence. Take the example of anti-Semitic pogroms, which can stand in for all racist violence. What the perpetrators of pogroms find intolerable and rage-provoking, what they react to, is not the immediate reality of Jews, but to the image/figure of the 'Jew' which circulates and has been constructed in their tradition. The catch, of course, is that one single individual cannot distinguish in any simple way between real Jews and their anti-Semitic image: this image over-determines the way I experience real Jews themselves and, furthermore, it affects the way Jews experience themselves. What makes a real Jew that an anti-Semite encounters on the street "intolerable," what the anti-Semite tries to destroy when he attacks the Jew, the true target of his fury, is this fantasmatic dimension.[12]

Rituality in the Ambedkarite Movement in Maharashtra

While the idea of "rituality" is central to anthropology, especially in culture studies, and while this idea is of extreme importance in understanding the Ambedkar movement in Maharashtra, with special reference to the personality cult where like Stalin who portrayed both himself and Lenin as the great heroes of the Bolshevik revolution (devaluing Trotsky, Bukharin, Zinoviev, Kamenev and the entire leadership of the 1917 revolution), Ambedkar is raised to the level of hero (despite Ambedkar's own idea of being against hero worship).[13] Consequently, what is noticed that instead of the political paradigm that Ambedkar himself had offered as an alternative to both the Congress and the Communist ones, the Ambekar movement by and large follows the level of hero worship. Ambedkar thus in the last resort turns out to be some sort of Stalin of Maharashtra. It is ironic that the one that hated deities, himself was raised to a deity by his followers.

Rationality is the exact opposite of rituality. In *Castes in India*, Ambedkar argued for "scientific explanation" as against religious validations.[14] While without doubts the idea of reason as it appears in the philosophy of the European Enlightenment is central to Ambedkar, the same cannot be said about his followers. Reason means essentially a faculty of critically inquiry and continuous questioning. There is nothing sacred before the altar of reason. The debate between Ambedkar and Gandhi was based on the issues of rituality and rationality. Ambedkar chose the latter path.

Understanding the Ambedkarite movement in Maharashtra, implies not only understanding social formations and the imagined category of caste suddenly emerging in the times of colonial capitalism and the emergence of subaltern politics by Jotiba Phule followed by Ambedkar's venture, but also understanding what happens post-Ambedkar, i.e. after 1957. Everything happening thenceforth is derivative of this.

The B.C. Kamble vs. Dadasaheb Gaikwad "issue" in the very year of Ambedkar's death forms the corpus of Ambedkar politics in Maharashtra even today. In 1957 the very year that Ambedkar died the Republican Party of India (RPI) split in two factions–the one that argued for the "correct" line (*durust*) and the "incorrect" line (*nadurust*). The incorrect line was that of agitation, so said B.C. Kamble. And since the Constitution was given by Ambedkar (so the Ambedkarite legend goes), all agitations would be deemed to be meaningless. What the Kamble line forgot was that in 1953 itself Ambedkar lamented that the provisions in the Constitution would benefit only a small section of the Dalits, that to from the cities and these beneficiaries would form a part of the consumerist middle class totally alienated from the movement for democratic change, large section of the Dalits would not be affected by merely depending on the provisions of the Constitution and forgetting political initiatives like *satyagrahas*. Despite Kamble having few takers in the Republican movement, it was his ideology of reconciling with the ruling Congress Party that would ultimately not only prevail in the Ambedkarite movement in Maharashtra, but would set the footprints for the future. One will have to see whether this complete dependence of the Congress and their appropriation of the Dalit movement would be complete and final. For Ambedkar as he asks:

> Had the Untouchables gone over to the Congress? Such a thing to me would be unimaginable. For, I could not believe that the Untouchables–apart from a few agents of the Congress who are always tempted by the Congress gold to play the part of the traitor–could think of going over to the Congress *en masse* forgetting how Mr. Gandhi and the Congress opposed, inch by inch up to the very last moment, every one of their demands for political safeguard.[15]

Note what Ambedkar says–the traitors who have been tempted by the Congress gold could go over to the Congress. For him, the Congress is essentially a party of upper caste elites who would never go for social reforms. Social reforms are necessary, but the Congress would at every moment be an impediment for the realisation of the same. It must be noted here that the first chapter of the same book–*What Congress and Gandhi Have Done to the Untouchables*– Ambedkar titles 'A Strange Event. Congress Takes Cognizance of the Untouchables'.[16]

It is this paradox facing the Ambedkar movement. One is then compelled to recall the German bard Goethe:

> Two souls alas, are housed within my breast,
> And each will wrestle for the mastery there.[17]

So what are the two souls that dwell in the breast of the Ambedkarite movement in Maharashtra? One is most certainly that of a passive and submissive form dictated by the Congress type of patronising politics where instead of actually being involved in the uplift of the subaltern masses and involving radical social reform project, co-opted the subaltern masses for political goals detrimental to both the subaltern masses and to the nation at large. But who dwells in the other part of the Faustian soul?

In January 2018 in the two hundredth year celebration of the victory of the forces that led to the collapse of the Peshwa rule in 1818 violence took place at Bhima Koregaon, the place that the battle took place giving way for British rule in Maharashtra. While fingers were pointed to certain right-wing groups for instigating violence, more fingers were pointed to the banned Communist Party if India (Maoist) followed by subsequent arrests of activists including that of the celebrated Ambedkar scholar Anand Teltumbde whose repertoire ranges from the articles penned for *Economic & Political Weekly* (under the idea 'Margins Speak')–now discontinued under the editorship of Gopal Guru (another Ambedkar scholar)–to *Mahad. The Making of the First Dalit Revolt*, *Republic of Caste* and the introduction to Ambedkar's *India and Communism*. The twist to the politics of the Ambedkar movement in Maharashtra would take a very different kind of "turn". Unlike the different "turns" that 20th century philosophy has taken–the "linguistic turn", etc.–this turn would state that there is something much more than social reform that the question would entail and this time it would go beyond the control of the Orientalists, colonial and post-colonial thinkers.

What is ironical is at no time did the Maoist movement in India starting in the 1960s ever taken the caste question seriously. For then it was the peasantry and the proletariat along with the middle class and the national bourgeoisie that would form the bloc of four classes which would lead the New Democratic revolution as they would call it after the classical Maoist fashion. Like the Communist Party of India and the Community Party of India (Marxist), caste was never an issue of such importance that would attract their attention. But if this is the case, then why did they get involved in the 2018 Bhima Koregaon incident, if indeed they did?

From a certain kind of "left" understanding, it is Anand Teltumbde who is probably one of the most serious in articulating the "Dalit" perspective. Incidentally he belongs to the Ambedkar family, married to Ambedkar's grandson Prakash Ambedkar's sister. Here it must be pointed out that Teltumbde because of his Marxist articulation is not considered as a part of the orthodox Ambedkar movement. In *Scripting the Change* a book edited by him based on essays written by the late Anuradha Ghandy a member of the banned Communist Party of India (Maoist), we find Ghandy's essay 'Caste Question in India'. According to her:

> The caste system has been one of the specific problems of the Indian democratic revolution. It is linked to the specific nature of the evolution of Indian society and has been one of the most important means for the exploitation of the labouring masses. Sanctioned by the Brahmanical Hindu religion, *Varnashrama Dharma* legitimised the oppression of the working people, and the enslavement and degradation of one section of the masses, reducing them to a near animal existence. For the ruling classes in India, from the ancient the modern period, the caste system served both as an ideology as well as a social system that enabled them to repress and exploit the majority of toilers.[18]

While claiming to use the Marxist method she further says that aim of the non-Brahman movement that Jotiba Phule had initiated in the 1870s she talks of "the non-Brahmans conscious of their exploitation by the Brahmans."[19] At least for the Marxist political economy where the idea of "exploitation" fits in, exploitation involves the extraction of surplus and in the labour process. Clearly, Ghandy is using the method that is at least alien to Marxism while arguing from the Maoist perspective. Instead what we see is a clear postmodern perspective where she combines caste and gender with the classical class question. But this does not work.

One of the important reasons for the RPI splitting in 1957 was that Gaikwad was seen to be close to Marxism. Kamble's alleged "only Constitutionalism" stems from his dislike for revolutionary methods. In the Ambedkarite movement in Maharashtra there has been a love-hate relation between the Ambedkarites and Marxists. One reason is that this antagonism has been because the Marxists from the time of S.A. Dange–the legendary communist leader from Bombay (now Mumbai)–probably did not understand what Ambedkar was theoretically, scientifically and politically proposing. Theoretically the Indian Marxists thought that for Marx only class mattered and the question of caste was being raised to nullify the class struggle which the Indian leftists thought would usher in communism. Clearly the Indian left was brought on only a partial reading of Marx's works. For one, Marx's *Ethnological Notebooks* was published by Lawrence Krader only in the 1970s and the founders of the left movement in India were totally oblivious of this work.

But one thing must be pointed out–the Indian left (like the Congress Party) treated Ambedkar very shabbily which is one reason for the Ambedkarites to dislike the Indian left. Scientifically it must be noted that there has been use and abuse of caste by the followers of Ambedkar. These said followers in the name of "social reform" follow electoral politics that serves what Kanshi Ram called the "era of stooges" where what one calls "politics" is made subservient to the politics of patron and client. In fact what the Ambedkarites in Maharashtra have not understood that Ammbedkar wanted to break out from this very politics of patron-client.

J.V. Pawar (one of the founders of the Dalit Panther movement in Maharashtra in the 1960s) in his five volumes on the *Ambedkarite Movement After Ambedkar* in Marathi offers an insider's perspective of the Ambedkar movement after Ambedkar. A startling comparison with the death of Lenin must be pointed out. Yet this comparison is also with extreme differences between the communist movement in Russia and the Soviet Union (post-Lenin) and the Ambedkarite movement post-Ambedkar. What is common is that extreme differences between Trotsky and Stalin. But what is different that Stalin massacred all his comrades, a feature that did not happen in India after the death of Ambedkar. What happened after Ambedkar is that extreme bickering happened which would continue to haunt the movement.

Religion and the Ambedkar Movement

One way to exorcise the ghosts of this bickering was to move into the realm of religion. A detailed analysis of Ambedkar's conversion to Buddhism has to be noted. C. Sheela Reddy[20] takes Ambedkar's views on religion, particularly his reasons for renouncing Hinduism, the religion of his birth. The well known narrative is that Ambedkar was born in an "untouchable" family and he struggled against untouchability and its stigmas. *Round Table India. For An Informed Age*, an Ambedkarite organisation promotes and propagates his ideas. The main question that is raised is that why did Ambedkar convert to Buddhism considering that he formed the Independent Labour Party in 1936 (15th August) and that his scientific training was a Fabian socialist trained by John Dewey at Columbia University? *Round Table India. For An Informed Age* says the following:

> A detailed answer to this question can be obtained by studying his The *Buddha and His Dhamma, Annihilation of Caste, Philosophy of Hinduism, Riddles in Hinduism*, etc. Nonetheless, some of his articles, speeches and interviews before and after his conversion to Buddhism throw some light on this question.... Ambedkar's statement in 1935 at the Yeola Conference is quite instructive in this regard. Ambedkar believed that the untouchables occupied a "weak and lowly status" only because they were a part of the Hindu society. When attempts to gain equal status and "ordinary rights as human beings" within the Hindu society started failing, Ambedkar thought it was essential to embrace a religion which will give "equal status, equal rights and fair treatment" to untouchables.

In his article 'Buddha and the Future of His Religion' published in 1950 in the *Mahabodhi Society Journal*, Ambedkar has summarised his views on religion and on Buddhism in the following manner:

1. The society must have either the sanction of law or the sanction of morality to hold it together. Without either, the society is sure to go to pieces.
2. Religion, if it is to survive, it must be in consonance with reason, which is another name for science.
3. It is not enough for religion to consist of a moral code, but its moral code must recognise the fundamental tenets of liberty, equality and fraternity.
4. Religion must not sanctify or make a virtue out of poverty

In May 1956, a talk by Ambedkar titled "Why I like Buddhism and how it is useful to the world in its present circumstances" was broadcast from the British Broadcasting Corporation, London. In his talk Ambedkar said:

> I prefer Buddhism because it gives three principles in combination, which no other religion does. Buddhism teaches *prajna* (understanding as against superstition and supernaturalism), *karuna* (love), and *samata* (equality). This is what man wants for a good and happy life. Neither god nor soul can save society.

In his last speech delivered in Bombay on May 24, 1956, in which he declared his resolve to embrace Buddhism, Ambedkar observed:

> Hinduism believes in God. Buddhism has no God. Hinduism believes in soul. According to Buddhism, there is no soul. Hinduism believes in *Chaturvarnya* and the caste system. Buddhism has no place for the caste system and *Chaturvarnya*.[21]

What must be said is that the binary that dominated colonial thinking–west/east, rational/irrational, scientific/mystical, Brahman/Shudra also seems to enter the Ambedkarite movement. The Hindu/Buddhism binary is one such example. The question then needs being posed is: "How much of colonial ethnography was present in Ambedkar's works?" Why did he not build the labour movement, since the depressed classes would be part of labour itself? The *Manifesto* of the Independent Labour Party mentions caste only once. In fact it is said that for him:

> Really seen here are only two castes in the world–the first, that of the rich, and the second of the poor.[22]

Critics could claim that Ambedkar did not put the idea of political economy and relate this with the social question of justice and dignity as he ought to have. But this would miss the main question that Ambedkar had–namely the question of human emancipation itself. On May 31, 1936 at Dadar, Bombay (now Mumbai) a year after the Yeole Conference where Ambedkar famously said, "I solemnly assure you that I will not die a Hindu," the following statements were displayed which reflects Ambedkar's ideology at that time.

> Man is not for religion, religion is for man.
>
> To become humans convert yourselves.
>
> To get organised convert yourselves.
>
> To achieve strength, convert yourselves.
>
> To secure liberty, convert yourselves.
>
> To make your domestic life happy, convert yourself.[23]

In this Conference, incidentally called only for the Mahar caste, Ambedkar attempted to answer why other depressed communities were not invited. He talks of "only of the Mahars" viz-a-vis "all the Untouchables"/"common meeting of all the Untouchables".[24] He also says:

> Though the other communities are not included they are not at loss.[25]

A critic could raise the question: "Was Ambedkar not following a policy of exclusion, where non-Mahar subaltern castes were not invited?" Kindly note:

> The other communities from the Untouchables are free to hold meetings like the Mahars and express their opinion. I would advise them to hold such meetings, and I will extend whatever help is needed from me, to the best of my capacity.[26]

This was in 1937. Today even in 2019 the Ambedkarite movement is not merely dominated Mahars, but is a Mahar movement. The

Chamaars and the Matangs refuse to be part of this movement, except for a few exceptions. The question of conversion could then be treated not as a critique of the caste system and the alleged excessive rituality surrounding the practice of Hinduism, but a messianic act. In the 1944 talk in Madras (now Chennai) which now appears as a small text *Indian History is Nothing But Struggle Between Buddhism and Brahmanism* he said that:

> The Buddhists were revolutionaries and Brahmans were counter-revolutionaries.[27]

The act of conversion was thus a messianic revolutionary act. After Alan Badiou one calls this an "Event". Ambedkarism thus has to be seen as some sort of messianism. In 1936 at Wardha he said the following:

> I do not promote Islam or Christian religions to anybody as yet. If anybody with his own responsibility promotes Islam or any other religion, he will be cheated for which I shall not be responsible. It is a fact that I have declared about conversion. But I have not said to adopt any particular religion as yet. Till that time all should carry out propaganda about conversion but they should not propagate any particular religion. When I declare, then only we all seven crore Untouchables convert at a time.[28]

While clearly Ambedkar's works like *Castes in India*, *Annihilation of Caste*, *Who Were the Shudras*, *India and Communism*, *What Congress and Gandhi Have Done to the Untouchables*, *Philosophy of Hinduism*, *Revolution and Counterrevolution in Ancient India*, *Buddha or Karl Marx*, are works of great scholarly importance, one cannot deny the fact that the Ambedkar movement in Maharashtra is basically a Mahar movement and that other subaltern castes have remained far away from it, in fact have also been antithetical to it. What could this reason be? And why did Ambedkar move from the Independent Labour Party (ILP) which is founded in 1936 and the Scheduled Castes Federation (SCF) founded in 1942 which later evolved into the Republican Party of India (RPI) finally converting to Buddhism? Was there an "epistemological break" in Ambedkar and has the Ambedkarite movement in Maharashtra been subject to this epistemological break? This work has attempted to see whether this term invented by Gaston Bachelard later taken over by Louis Althusser can actually function in understanding both Ambedkar and the Ambedkarite movement in Maharashtra? Further, this work has also tried to document how much Ambedkar was influenced by socialism (both Fabian and Marxism) and whether these influences were ever present in the Ambedkarite movement in Maharashtra. It must be noted that in 1956 one year before Ambedkar's death he started a 'Training School for Entrance to Politics' which was to train cadres for the Republican Party of India (RPI). However the first batch of the school was also the last batch. Clearly the theoretical direction that Ambedkar himself wanted to give the RPI was not successful. Ambedkar seems to have been betrayed by his followers.

Ambedkar's vision was vast. He wanted all the oppressed to accept his vision of emancipation. His embracing of Buddhism then is not seen as a mechanical reaction to Hinduism and the caste system, but an alternative *Weltanschauung* that could synthesise diverse theoretical problematics including that of socialism.

Was Ambedkar a Socialist?

While the Ambedkar movement in Maharashtra has always stayed far away from the ideology of socialism, especially all RPI factions, for Ambedkar the labour question was tantamount for him. In his *States and Minorities: What Are Their Rights and How to Secure Them in the Constitution of Free India* (a speech delivered in March 1947 and published in May 1947) is said to be "at his radical left-leaning best–a tendency he was to curtail in the Constituent Assembly of India where other members of the drafting committee did not favour such a radical tenor."[29] According to Ambedkar the Indian Constitution had to relate politics with the socio-economic terrain. Thus:

> What is the nature of the Indian constitution which is on the anvil? This of course raises another question. What should be the nature of the Constitution? Should it be a Constitution

> which should prescribe the political structure of the society or should it go further and prescribe the social and economic structure of society as well? A constitution which is purely political stops with prescribing the various organs of the state, namely the legislature, the executive and the judiciary, their interrelation, the franchise, recruitment to public services and frequency of election to the legislatures. A constitution which is politico-socio-economic, besides prescribing the nature of the various organs of the state, also proceeds to prescribe a particular form of an economic organisation of the society. That is to say prescribes the ownership of the management of the instruments of production and the distribution of the income among the members of the society.[30]

Clearly Ambedkar is against the liberal argument that liberty and equality are in contradistinction with one another and that economic guarantees do not take away the liberty of the individual.[31] For him there is what Etienne Balibar calls "eqa-liberty". "Indeed", so he goes on, "the safeguarding of individual liberty requires that the constitution should prescribe the economic shape of society."[32]

Not only is Ambedkar a socialist, he is a socialist who is an outright anti-capitalist. Thus:

> Anyone who studies the working of the system of social economy based on private enterprise and the pursuit of personal gain will realise how it undermines, if it does not actually violate, the last two premises on which democracy rests (i.e. that the individual shall not be required to relinquish any of his constitutional rights as a condition precedent to the receipt of a privilege and that the state shall not delegate powers to private persons to govern others).[33]

Consequently: "How many have to relinquish their liberty in order to gain their living? How many have to subject themselves to be governed by private employers? Ask those who are unemployed whether their liberty is of any value to them."[34] As for the proponents of laissez faire economics "liberty from the control of the state is another name for the dictatorship of the private employer."[35] His concept of political economy is planned economy which is permanent.[36] And against the grain of thought that classifies Ambedkar as a liberal and a supporter of parliamentary democracy (Christophe Jaffrelot follows this line of thinking)[37] one should recall Ambedkar once again who says that economic betterment of society "cannot be secured under the form of government called parliamentary democracy."[38] Consequently:

> There is great need of someone with sufficient courage to tell Indians: "Beware of parliamentary democracy; it is not the best product as it appears to be."[39]

For parliamentary democracy "has continuously added to the economic wrongs of the poor, the downtrodden and the disinherited class."[40]

While being a critique of capitalism, Ambedkar clearly was not for the Soviet Union type of communism because he thought that it was a thoughtless state which while securing economic stability destroyed the liberty of the individual.[41] It is here that one needs to go into contemporary post-Marxist discourse which has articulated the theme close to Ambedkar's heart, namely the relation between equality and liberty. Accordingly to Balibar, the idea of equaliberty combines equality and liberty such that there is "no equality without liberty, no liberty without equality."[42] Orthodox Marxism for Ambedkar could not offer a solution to either the crisis of capitalism or of caste-based society. Thus to the question that Ambedkar himself poses: "Can labour choose communism?" he himself answers: "I think it cannot. For under communism, workers may get equality with the erstwhile class owners but they are sure to lose their rights to liberty."[43] Ambedkar does not go into the crimes of Stalin and Stalinism and how it created not a communist society but the most despicable form of totalitarian-despotic society. He does not go into the fake Moscow Trials of the late 1930s where Stalin literally killed all members of the central committee at the time of the 1917 Bolshevik Revolution and Lenin's close associates leaving only himself (Stalin) to rule.[44]

For Ambedkar socialism had to be an enlightened-libertarian type of socialism that had to leave behind the core Marxist categories, especially that of the dictatorship of the proletariat that Marx himself introduced in his *Critique of Gotha Programme.* In this sense, Ambedkar was a post-Marxist thinker well before the European intelligentsia introduced this to the world.

Ambedkar and Constitutional Fetishism

We go back to Kamble's Constitutionalism and his disavowal of agitational methods. In fact what we call "Ambedkarite politics in general" in Maharashtra as "Ambedkarite politics from above" is by and large a Constitutional fetish politics which then turns into the most crude form of identity politics. By fetish we mean the compulsive attachment (Freud's idea of "obsessional attachment") to a non-existing object. And by Constitutional fetishism we mean obsessional attachment to the Constitution that actually is more absent than present. We call this after the language of postmodernism as "absent present". We derive this term from Jacques Derrida.

But this must be contextualised properly. It was Arun Shourie who in his *Worshipping False Gods, Ambedkar and the Facts Which Have Been Erased* called Ambedkar the "false Manu" (literally the false and duplicate lawmaker).[45] For Shourie, Ambedkar played no major role in the shaping of the Constitution, for the Ambedkarites it is exactly otherwise–Ambedkar was the author of the entire Constitution and not the head of the Drafting Committee responsible for drafting the Constitution (which in fact he was). Iconic images and statues all over India of Ambedkar one arm pointing to the sky and one with a book (the Indian Constitution) follow the messianic line that he, and he alone, was responsible for the Constitution.

Jaffrelot has a more balanced view. For him, "If Ambedkar was not the author of the Constitution, he was always at hand throughout its formulation."[46] Further he was involved in "repeatedly shaping the debates" and "therefore played a determining role in the shaping of India's Constitution..."[47] Reading the Constitutional Assembly Debates we see that Ambedkar as a staunch socialist becomes some sort of "free thinker". Though even in these debates the question of economic democracy came up and even when he (Ambedkar) reiterated the importance of economic democracy bringing in the notions of capitalism, socialism and communism, he brings in "free choice" in this new matrix. Thus:

> As I stated, our Constitution as a piece of mechanism lays down what is called parliamentary democracy. By parliamentary democracy we mean 'one man, one vote'. We also mean that every government shall be on the anvil, both in its daily affairs and also at the end of a certain period when the voters and the electorate will be given an opportunity to assess the work done by the government. The reason why we have established in this Constitution a political democracy is because we do not install by any means whatsoever a perpetual dictatorship of any particular body of the people. While we have established political democracy, it is also the desire that we should lay down as our ideal economic democracy. We do not want merely to lay down a mechanism to enable people to come and capture power. The Constitution also wishes to lay down an ideal before those who would be forming the government. That idea is economic democracy, whereby, so far as I am concerned, I understand to mean, 'one man, one vote'. The question is: Have we got any fixed idea as to how we should bring about economic democracy? There are various ways in which people believe that economic democracy can be brought about; there are those who believe in individualism as the best form of economic democracy; there are those who believe in having a socialistic state as the best form of economic democracy; there are those who believe in the communistic idea as the most perfect form of economic democracy.
>
> Now, having regard to the fact that there are various ways by which economic democracy may be brought about, we have deliberately introduced in the language that we have used, in the directive principles, something which is not fixed or rigid. We have left enough room for people of different ways of thinking, with regard to the reaching of the ideal of economic democracy, to strive in their own way, to persuade the electorate that it is the best way of reaching economic democracy, the fullest opportunity to act in the way in which they want to act.

> Sir, that is the reason why the language of the articles in Part IV is left in the manner in which this Drafting Committee thought it best to leave it. It is no use giving a fixed, rigid form to something which is not rigid, which is fundamentally changing and must, having regard to the circumstances and the times, keep on changing. It is, therefore, no use saying that the directive principles have no value. In my judgment, the directive principles have a great value, for they lay down that our ideal is economic democracy. Because we did not want merely a parliamentary form of government to be instituted through the various mechanisms provided in the Constitution, without any direction as to what our economic ideal, as to what our social order ought to be, we deliberately included the Directive Principles in our Constitution. I think, if the friends who are agitated over this question bear in mind what I have said just now that our object in framing this Constitution is really two fold: (i) to lay down the form of political democracy, and (ii) to lay down that our ideal is economic democracy and also to prescribe that every government whatever, it is in power, shall strive to bring about economic democracy, much of the misunderstanding under which most members are labouring will disappear.[48]

Jaffrelot interprets this section where he depicts Ambedkar as a liberal democrat who even opposes the constitutional amendment to nationalise natural resources.[49] In contrast one turns to Ambedkar's intervention in 1946, at the first meeting that took place on December 9. It once again was on the question of socialism. Consider Ambedkar who says that:

> ...there are here certain provisions which speak of justice–economic, social and political....(It is) expected (that) the Resolution to state in the most explicit terms that, in order that they may be social and economic justice in this country, there would be nationalisation of industry and nationalisation of land. I do not understand how it could be possible for any future government to believe in doing justice–socially, economically and politically–unless its economy is a socialist economy.[50]

Further In his *States and Minorities*, Ambedkar says:

The United States of India shall declare as a part of the law of the Constitution–

1. That industries which are key industries or which may be declared to be key industries shall be owned and run by the State.
2. That industries which are not key industries but which are basic industries shall be owned by the State and shall be run by the State or by Corporations established by the State.
3. That Insurance shall be a monopoly of the State.
4. That agriculture shall be State industry.
5. That State shall acquire the subsisting rights in such industries, insurance and agricultural land held by private individuals.

9. Agricultural industry shall be organised on the following basis:
   (i) The State shall divide the land acquired into farms of standard size and let out the farms for cultivation to residents of the village as tenants (made up of groups of families) to cultivate on the following conditions: (a) The farm shall be cultivated as a collective farm, (b) The farm shall be cultivated in accordance with rules and directions issued by government, (c) The tenants shall share among themselves in the manner prescribed the produce of the farm left after the payment of charges properly leviable on the farm.
   (ii) The land shall be let out to villagers without distinction of caste or creed and in such manner there will be no landlord, no tenant and no landless labourer.
   (iii) It shall be the obligation of the State to finance the cultivation of the collective farms by the supply of water, draft animals, implements, manure, seeds, etc.
10. The scheme shall be brought into operation as early as possible but in no case shall the period extend beyond the

> tenth year from the date of the Constitution coming into operation.[51]

The question that emerges is why did Ambedkar not insist on keeping these socialist ideas in the Constituent Assembly that could have given a socialist Constitution of India? Niraja Jayal in her *Citizenship and Its Discontents: An Indian History* analyses these issue of whether Ambedkar backtracked from his socialist position to the forgetfulness of socialism.[52]

The question is that if indeed Ambedkar had a clear socialist view of society where social, economic and political democracy went together, then why was the entire project of socialist concepts absent in the final Constitution of which he himself was Chairman of the Drafting Committee? Why was only protection of the weaker sections of society (SCs and STs) included but not the project of the annihilation of caste? And if indeed these ideas (annihilation of caste and realisation of socialism) were absent in the Constitution, then why this fetish of making Ambedkar as the author of a Constitution that was contra Ambedkar himself? Do we then find and Ambedkar contra Ambedkar?

Consider Jaffrelot who says that even though Ambedkar as a proponent of politico-socio-economic democracy he "opposed a constitutional amended to nationalise natural resources."[53] This according to Jaffrelot was Ambedkar's "attachment to liberal democracy."[54]

The question that one needs to be posed is: "Was Ambedkar a socialist as clearly shown right till his 1947 States and Minorities or was he a liberal democrat? In fact the entire Ambedkarite movement in Maharashtra is haunted with this dilemma. The RPI split in 1957 which broke the Maharashtra in the Kamble vs. Gaikwad line is based on this binary–socialism/liberalism. The two souls in the post-Ambedkar Ambedkarite movement would continue to haunt the movement of politico-socio-economic democracy.

For Ambedkar there are two types of emancipation–political, which is partial and the other which is a "universal emancipation of society."[55] Marx thought that it was the proletariat which is the bearer of this universal human emancipation, since it is a universal class representing universal suffering.[56] It is the "universal representative."[57]

Ambedkar, Gandhi and Nehru

It is probably in 1932 with relation to Ambedkar's affirmation of separate electorates for the then Untouchables and Gandhi's firm opposition stating that the Hindus would be fragmented if separate electorates would be implemented. The issue that emerges is complex or borrowing the terminology of Sigmund Freud's *Interpretation of Dreams* which the French structuralist Louis Althusser kept central in his *For Marx*, we have an overdetermination where reality is described as "complexly-structurally unevenly determined".

What we intend to say is that one cannot simply make a metaphysical opposition: Hindus vs. Untouchables, Gandhi vs. Ambedkar. Instead we have besides these two tall leaders, also Madan Mohan Malaviya, B.S Moonje (a Hindu Mahasabha leader) and M.C. Rajah (a Tamil Dalit leader who opposed Ambedkar in his politics of conversion)–the latter two being instrumental in having the 1932 Rajah-Moonje Pact which is supposed to have formed the guidelines for the Poona Pact (which Gandhi ironically never signed).[58] The social and political reality emerging hereon (post 1932) deals with not only Ambedkar and Gandhi, but also this complexly-structurally unevenly determined reality where manifold jati-communities were struggling to find their voices in an emerging democratic atmosphere.

While on the one hand it seems that the demand for separate electorates for the subalterns castes was a revolutionary step, on the other hand it is obvious that it would break the unity of the popular classes and strengthen the British policy of divide and rule. One must point out that Ambedkar was not alone in trying to address the caste system. Clearly Gandhi was also involved and with the help of his capitalist friend G.D. Birla financed Gandhi's pet project–All India Anti-Untouchability League.[59]

Yet it must be stated that the line of demarcation between them was very deep. For Ambedkar, "no matter what Hindus say, Hinduism is a menace to liberty, equality and fraternity"[60] and "the

Mahatma appears not to believe in thinking. He prefers to follow the saints."[61]

What we are saying is that we do not live in the era of "development", most certainly not in the era of economic, cultural, national and human development, but in the age of the destruction of reason and humanity. The crucial site for the Indian counterrevolution is caste, which has destroyed human creativity, humanity and individuality. This neither Gandhi, nor Nehru ever recognised. Both were celebrators of the caste system. Note Gandhi's statement that "the caste system has saved Hinduism from disintegration" as he had noted in his 'The Caste System' (1920).[62] Also note that Gandhi was in actuality no apostle of peace. This is a fiction made by the colonialists to construct the figure of non-violence in order to negate all possibilities of revolutionary action against British rule in India. It also must be noted (which Perry Anderson highlights in *The Indian Ideology* and which I have brought out in *Yusuf and Zuleika* that for Gandhi ahimsa is a pure fiction and that "all killing is not *himsa*" as he said in his 'Letter to Hanumantrao', July 17, 1918.[63] For Gandhi (one could say that this parallels the idea of Heinrich Himmler, Hitler's deputy) that he who "alone can practise *ahimsa* who knows how to kill" as he noted in his 'Speech at Ras', June 26, 1918.[64] The Mahatma went on (again note the Nazi echoes on violence and non-violence): "You cannot teach *ahimsa* to a man who cannot kill. You cannot make a dumb man appreciate the beauty and the merit of silence" as he writes in the 'Letter to C.F. Andrews' June 23, 1918[65] and the "practice of *ahimsa* may even necessitate killing and that we as a nation have lost the true power of killing. It is clear", so the Mahatma went on "that he who has lost the power to kill cannot practise non-killing. *Ahimsa* is a renunciation of the highest type" in his 'Letter to Hanumantrao', July 17, 1918.[66]

Not only did Gandhi preach the strange, in fact very violent form of the metaphysics of ahimsa, he was clearly on the side of the propertied class. Consider him telling the landlords in 'Answers to Zamindars' [July 25, 1934]: "I shall be no party to dispossessing propertied classes of their private property without just cause... But supposing that there is an attempt unjustly to deprive you of your property, you will find me fighting on your side."[67] It is clear from this that Gandhi was a supporter of the zamindars and feudal landed property. It is in this site of "agent" that we need to see Gandhi. Modern renderings of Gandhi (Ramchandra Guha is one example) completely miss out this point of Gandhi as mediator and agent, in fact as transcendental mediator. Just as Christ appeared as the fantastic mediator between god and humanity, and the state appears as a mediator between the capitalists and the proletariat so too Gandhi appears as the mediator "working for the cooperation and coordination of capital and labour and of landlords and tenants.[68]

Gandhi was a spiritualist in the very bad sense of the term. Ambedkar said that while Gandhi tried to "spiritualise politics", he in fact actually commercialised not only politics and spirituality, but commercialised himself.[69] The movement against the British was because he (Gandhi) wanted to free "my soul from the bondage of flesh."[70] The freedom movement was merely a means for Gandhi to obtain this freedom from transcendental bondage. Gandhi said that he did not think that he was a prophet[71], yet it is the mantle of the "Mahatma" that he took with great ease. He tried his best to be the apostle of peace and Hindu-Muslim fraternity, but his views on Muslims were not exactly encouraging. Note how for him, "The Mussulman being generally in a minority has as a class developed into a bully.....(where) thirteen thousand years of imperialistic expansion has made the Mussulmans fighters as a body. They are therefore aggressive. Bullying is the natural excrescence of an aggressive spirit."[72] What "imperialist expansion"! What is Gandhi saying? And if he is so concerned about imperialism and imperialist expansion why was he working according to the logic of colonialism and the myths of imperialism–namely that Islam is violent and imperialist?

Further why does Gandhi oppose "Hinduism" and "Islam"? Was he then no different from the founders of Hindutva, namely Savarkar and Golwalkar? Gandhi was no different from the ideologues of Hindutva. Note how he considers Hindus as "essentially non-violent."[73]

Both Gandhi and Nehru had influences of European romanticism in their respective politics. When Nehru said that caste was to be considered as a type of "joint family"[74], not only was he mistaken, he was scientifically incorrect. But then it must be noted that it was not just the European romanticists who saw the Indian caste system as a form of democratic collective; it was also the Nazis who were enamoured by caste. In my *Yusuf and Zuleika*, where I have highlighted the romanticisation of the Gandhi-Nehru duo, I have said that unlike Ambedkar who in his *Castes in India* saw caste as an "enclosed class"[75], Nehru understood caste as "an all-inclusive order without any common dogma and allowing the fullest latitude to each group"[76] even a form of "trade unions or craft-guilds" governed by a "strong sense of solidarity."[77] Nehru imagined that he had "distinctive Aryan features",[78] while Gandhi was (as Perry Anderson notes in his *The Indian Ideology*) a "cross between a Jain-infected Hindu orthodoxy and late Victorian psychomancy, the world of Madame Blavatsky, Theosophy, *planchette* and the Esoteric Christian Union" where cruxification of the flesh along with the phantasmagoria of celibacy would govern his politics.[79]

But as I have said in my *Yusuf and Zuleika* that both Gandhi and Nehru were schooled in western theosophy. It is pertinent to note (as Perry Anderson points out) that Annie Besant herself performed the ceremony of initiation for the young teenaged Nehru.[80]

Tarrying with the Mundane

Tarrying with the Negative. Kant, Hegel, and the Critique of Ideology is a book by Slavoj Žižek. We have transposed this idea as "Tarrying with the Mundane". Clearly post-Ambedkar scholarship has been either partisan or mundane to the extreme where instead of destroying caste and its traumatic excess, this duo (caste and its traumas) have been rehabilitated in the liberal democratic framework. And it is the mundane which matters more than the partisan. To be more explicit we should look at the following:

Ambedkar's final aim was to integrate the Dalits into an egalitarian Indian society as an indistinguishable part of it with the same social status and rights as the rest. He would never do anything which would jeopardise the prospect of such a society emerging through the combined efforts of all. The rationalism which Ambedkar adopted was the rationalism of the enlightenment The principal elements in it were (i) the concept of the scientific method–the empirical method supplemented by the hypothetico-deductive method–as the only valid method of human knowledge and the corollary that the knowledge yielded by this method is the only valid form of human knowledge; (ii) the concept of a rational morality based on (a) the utilitarian criterion of a right action, viz. that an action is right if and only ** if the consequences which follow from it tend to satisfy the maximum possible human desires; and (b) the principle of egalitarian justice, viz. that the happiness or well-being (measured in terms of the number of his satisfied desires) of any person has as much worth as that of any other person. What is curious is that it is this rationalistic concept of secular morality which Ambedkar reads in Buddha's concept of *dhamma*. What is curious is that he further adds that morality must be regarded as 'Sacred'. 'Mere morality', he asserts is not enough. It must be sacred and 'Universal'." Ambedkar does make a valiant attempt to give a secular meaning to 'sacred'. He says, "When a thing or a belief has reached the stage of being sacred it means that it cannot be violated". But it is implied in calling a principle or a rule moral that it is inviolable; it ought not to be violated. And if all that is involved in calling morality sacred is that it is inviolable, surely the word is redundant. It is significant that Ambedkar felt obliged to insist that morality must be sacred. In spite of his rationalistic professions, Ambedkar could not altogether reject the transcendent dimension of human existence. For the Buddha the fruit of steadily living in the path of dhamma was 'Nibbana'. Nibbana consists in extinguishing the flame of individual existence by totally dissolving one's egoity, one's belief that one is a particular, enduring person, identical with oneself and distinct from others with one's own exclusive well-being to pursue in a situation of confrontation with others.

> The way to achieve *nibbana* is to cultivate self-knowledge, that one is merely a congeries and succession of passing phenomena without a hard self-identity and by practising the virtues of compassion, friendship, etc. Ambedkar, however, was not satisfied with *Dhamma*. He wanted it to be *Saddhamma*. This means he wanted *Dhamma* to bring about a social change and lead men to an ideal society. He wants to make the world a kingdom of righteousness.[81]

It is clear that post-Ambedkar no one could take on the mantle of either his scholarship or political morality. Ambedkar scholarship by and large follows the caste epistemology–those from the Mahar background become "Ambedkarites" and "Ambedkar scholars". Take the case of the 2013 publication of Hari Mohan Sharma (who calls himself "Dr. Hari Mohan Sharma) titled *Selected Speech of Dr. B.R. Ambedkar. His Life and Philosophy.* Clearly the title is wrong both in terms of context and grammar since he has taken major works like *Castes in India* and *Buddha or Marx* (which are not speeches).[82]

Tarrying with the mundane has ultimately left the post-Ambedkar Ambedkarite movement as being nothing but patrons of the major bourgeois political parties.

Revolutions are needed for human emancipation. And for this a revolution in ideas and the construction of a new language of politics is necessary. Both caste and its traumas can be expelled when a new language of politics and philosophy is constructed. Marx and Ambedkar both ignited philosophical revolutions in the realm of ideas. But these revolutions were subsumed in the networks of bourgeois ideology constructed by the ideology of modern caste oligarchy, the class system and the logic of capital accumulation. Modern India did not annihilate caste or capitalism; it refashioned both of them in the image of the Indian liberal order. Now fascism has come and is once again refashioning caste and capitalism.

Instead of having industries as the temples of modern India, we now have temples as the industries of fascist India. There is no alternative left. Earlier it was thought that a revolution in ideas is a *luxury* for the intellectuals. Now it is a *necessity*. The earlier worded old language is no longer going to be sufficient. We need a new language to be constructed for "language itself", to recall Žižek once again, "the very medium of non-violence, of mutual recognition, involves unconditional violence."[83] We live in the world of unconditional violence where non-violence has become another name for extreme and permanent violence.

And more than violence, it is non-violence that is killing us all.

Postscript

While the triumph of the Modi-led BJP government in the 2019 national elections is said to be a mutation from the Nehru-Gandhi paradigm, where the Savarkar-Golwalkar theoretical problematic is said to displace the former, a deeper analysis–mainly drawn from a revolutionary reading of Marx and Ambedkar–says that this triumph is a continuation of the Nehru-Gandhi paradigm. This essay thus says that making claims that there is a severe "epistemological break" between the Nehru-Gandhi paradigm and the Savarkar-Golwalkar political problematic is wrong, just as the claims that there is severe epistemological break between liberalism and fascism is wrong, since these are both forms of bourgeois rule and thus natural continuation of the politics of bourgeoisdom. In my book *Yusuf and Zuleika. The Return of the Despot*, I have said that there is no essential difference between liberalism and fascism and that liberalism is only fascism without a gun and fascism is liberalism with a gun.[84] Likewise it is quite unclear why liberalism is being hailed as to not only a form of ideal governance, but also as the solution to populism, authoritarianism and fascism. To this we turn to Samir Amin's *The Liberal Virus* and say that we are all infected by this liberal virus that has caused a curious form of schizophrenia that is leading humanity to its final holocaust.[85] Advocates of the Nehru-Gandhi form of governance claim that liberalism is now being swept away by the triumph of the Modi-led BJP government. But what they do not say is that for liberalism there are three things of great importance: (1) the disappearance of the socialist model, (2) the hegemonism of the United States, and (3) that the only economic system that can function is capitalism.[86]

It is in this perspective that one must stress that liberalism stands for the unquestioned triumph of capitalism and that there is absolutely no need for going into the Nehru-Savarkar, Gandhi-Godse debate. This debate is utterly false and the problem does not have to be solved, but dissolved. This chapter is on the dissolution of the false bourgeois problems. The underlying theme is that liberalism is nothing but fascism without a gun and fascism is liberalism with a gun.

References

1. See for instance Etienne Balibar, 'Foreword'. Althusser and the "Ideological State Apparatus", in Louis Althusser, *On the Reproduction of Capitalism. Ideology and Ideological State Apparatus*, trans. G.M. Goshgarian (London: Verso, 2014), p. XIII and Louis Althusser, 'Law', in Ibid., pp. 57-69.
2. Althusser, 'Law', in Ibid., p. 65.
3. V.I. Lenin, *Materialism and Empiro-criticism* (Moscow: Progress Publishers, 1975), p. 320.
4. Karl Marx and Frederick Engels, *The German Ideology* (Moscow: Progress Publishers, 1977), p. 254.
5. Karl Marx, 'The Eighteenth Brumaire of Louis Bonaparte', in *Marx. Engels. Selected Works*, (Moscow: Progress Publishers, 1975), p. 96.
6. Ibid.
7. Slavoj Žižek, 'Language, Violence and Non-violence', in *International Journal of Žižek Studies*, Vol. 2, No. 3, 2016.
8. Ibid. See also Jacques Lacan, *Ecrits* (Norton: New York, 2006), p. 276.
9. Slavoj Žižek, 'Language, Violence and Non-violence'.
10. Sigmund Freud, 'The Uncanny', in *The Penguin Freud Library. Vol. 14. Art and Literature* (London: Penguin Books, 1990), p. 339.
11. Slavoj Žižek, op. cit.
12. Ibid.
13. See B.R. Ambedkar, 'Castes in India', p. 255.
14. Ibid.

15. B.R. Ambedkar, 'What Congress and Gandhi have Done to the Untouchables', in *Dr. Babasaheb Ambedkar. Writings and Speeches*, Vol. 9 (Mumbai: Education Department, Government of Maharashtra, 2016), p. ii.
16. Ibid., pp. 1-17.
17. Johann Wolfang Von Goethe, *Faust*, Vol. I trans. Philip Wayne (London: Penguin, 1949), p. 67.
18. Anuradha Ghandy, 'Caste Question in India', in *Scripting the Change. Selected Writings of Anuradha Ghandy*, ed. Anand Teltumbde and Shoma Sen with forward by Arundhati Roy (Delhi: Daanish Books, 2011), p. 7.
19. Ibid., p. 35.
20. C. Sheela Reddy, 'Ambedkar's Work and Mission' in *Mainstream Journal*, April 12, 2008.
21. http://roundtableindia.co.in/index.php?option=com_content&view=article&id=1044:why-dr-ambedkar-renounced-hinduism&catid=116&Itemid=128.
22. See Christophe Jaffrelot, *Dr. Ambedkar and Untouchability: Analyzing and Fighting Caste* (London: Hurst and Co., 2005).
23. B.R. Ambedkar, 'What way Emancipation?', in *Dr. Babasaheb Ambedkar Writings and Speeches, Vol. 17, Part Three* (Bombay: Education Department, Government of Maharashtra, 1989), p. 113.
24. Ibid., p. 116.
25. Ibid.
26. Ibid.
27. B.R. Ambedkar, 'Indian History is Nothing but Struggle Between Buddhism and Brahmanism', in *Dr. Babasaheb Ambedkar Writings and Speeches, Vol. 17, Part Three, Dr. B.R. Ambedkar and the Egalitarian Revolution, Speeches* (Bombay: Education Department, Government of Maharashtra, 1989), p. 335.
28. B.R. Ambedkar, 'I Cannot Sacrifice My Conscience for Success', in *Dr. Babasaheb Ambedkar Writings and Speeches, Vol. 17, Dr. B.R. Ambedkar and the Egalitarian Revolution, Part Three, Speeches* (Bombay: Education Department, Government of Maharashtra, 1989), p. 105.

29. See note by S. Anand to B.R. Ambedkar, 'Labour and the Constitution', in *Thus Spoke Ambedkar, Vol. 1. A Stake in the Nation*, ed. Bhagwan Das (New Delhi: Navayana, 2010), p. 70.
30. B.R. Ambedkar, 'Labour and the Constitution', p. 71.
31. Ibid., p. 72.
32. Ibid., p. 73.
33. Ibid.
34. Ibid.
35. Ibid., p. 74.
36. Ibid., pp. 74-75.
37. See Christophe Jaffrelot, *Dr. Ambedkar and Untouchability*, p. 108.
38. Ibid.
39. B.R. Ambedkar, 'The Failures of Parliamentary Democracy', in *Thus Spoke Ambedkar, Vol. 1. A Stake in the Nation*, ed. Bhagwan Das (New Delhi: Navayana, 2010), p. 46.
40. Ibid., p. 47.
41. B.R. Ambedkar, 'Labour and the Constitution', in *Thus Spoke Ambedkar, Vol. 1. A Stake in the Nation*, ed. Bhagwan Das (New Delhi: Navayana, 2010), p. 76.
42. Etienne Balibar, *Politics and the Other Scene*, trans. Christine Jones, James Swenson and Chris Turner (London: Verso, 2002), p. 2.
43. B.R. Ambedkar, 'Labour and the Constitution', p. 76.
44. See my *In the Name of Marx* (Delhi: Aakar Books, 2018) and *Yusuf and Zuleika* (Delhi: Aakar Books, 2019) where I have analysed the crimes of Stalin and Stalinism and said that the Indian left could never exorcise the ghost of Stalinism that once governed them and yet governs them. Ambedkar was always opposed by the Indian Stalinists led by S.A. Dange and followed by B.T. Randive who saw Ambedkar as a British stooge.
45. See Arun Shourie, *Worshipping False Gods, Ambedkar and the Facts Which Have Been Erased* (New Delhi: ASA, 1997).
46. Christophe Jaffrelot, op. cit., p. 108.
47. Ibid.
48. See *Constitutional Assembly Debates*, Vol. VII, http://164.100.47.194/Loksabha/Debates/cadebatefiles/C19111948.html

49. Christophe Jaffrelot, op. cit., p. 109.
50. B.R. Ambedkar, 'The Need for a Unitary Government', in *Thus Spoke Ambedkar, Vol. 1. A Stake in the Nation*, ed. Bhagwan Das (New Delhi: Navayana, 2010), p. 151.
51. B.R. Ambedkar, *States and Minorities: What are their Rights and How to Secure Them in the Constitution*, in https://cadindia.clpr.org.in/historical_constitutions/states_and_minorities__dr__b_r__ambedkar__1945__1st%20January%201945. B.R. Ambedkar, 'States and Minorities', in *Dr. Babasaheb Ambedkar Writings and Speeches, Vol. 1* (Bombay: Education Department, Government of Maharashtra, 1989), p. 396.
52. Niraja Jayal, *Citizenship and Its Discontents: An Indian History* (Cambridge: Harvard University Press, 2013).
53. Christophe Jaffrelot, op. cit., p. 109.
54. Ibid.
55. See Karl Marx, 'Critique of Hegel's Philosophy of Right. Introduction', in *Karl Marx. Early Writings*, trans Rodney Livingstone (New York: Vintage Books, 1975), pp. 254-255.
56. Ibid., p. 254.
57. Ibid.
58. See Christophe Jafferlot, op. cit., p. 67.
59. Ibid.
60. B.R. Ambedkar, *Pakistan or the Partition of India* (Bombay, 1946), p. 354.
61. B.R. Ambedkar, 'Reply to the Mahatma', in *The Essential Writings of B.R. Ambedkar*, ed. Valerian Rodrigues (New Delhi: Oxford University Press, 2008), p. 318.
62. M.K. Gandhi, 'The Caste System' (1920) *Collected Works of Mahatma Gandhi*, Vol. 19 (Ahmedabad: The Publication Division, Ministry of Information and Broadcasting, Government of India, 1966), p. 83. See also Perry Anderson, *The Indian Ideology* (Gurgaon: Three Essays Collective, 2012), p. 37, n. 40.
63. M.K. Gandhi, 'Letter to Hanumantrao', July 17, 1918, in *Collected Works of Mahatma Gandhi*, Vol. 14 (Ahmedabad: The Publication Division, Ministry of Information and Broadcasting, Government of India, 1965), p. 485.

64. M.K. Gandhi, 'Speech at Ras', June 26, 1918 in *The Bombay Chronicle*, July 2, 1918, in *Collected Works of Mahatma Gandhi*, Vol. 14, p. 454.
65. M.K. Gandhi, 'Letter to C.F. Andrews' June 23, 1918, in *Collected Works of Mahatma Gandhi*, Vol. 14, p. 444.
66. M.K. Gandhi, 'Letter to Hanumantrao', July 17, 1918, in ibid., p. 485.
67. M.K. Gandhi, 'Answers to Zamindars' [July 25, 1934], in *The Penguin Gandhi Reader*, ed. Rudrangshu Mukherjee (New Delhi: Penguin Books, 1993), p. 238.
68. Ibid., pp. 238-240.
69. B.R. Ambedkar, Reply to the Mahatma', in *Essential Writings of B.R. Ambedkar*, ed. Valerian Rodrigues, p. 316.
70. M.K. Gandhi, 'My Mission', *Young India*, April 23, 1924, in Ibid., p. 17.
71. Ibid.
72. M.K. Gandhi, 'What May Hindus Do?", in *Young India*, June 19, 1924, in Ibid., p. 21.
73. Ibid., pp. 21-22.
74. Jawaharlal Nehru, *The Discovery of India* (London: Meridian Books Ltd., 1946), pp. 206-212.
75. See my *Yusuf and Zuleika: The Return of the Despot* (Delhi: Aakar Books, 2019). Also see B.R. Ambedkar, 'Castes in India, Their Mechanism, Genesis and Development", in *The Essential Writings of B.R. Ambedkar*, ed. Valerian Rodrigues (New Delhi: Oxford University Press, 2008), pp. 253, 257.
76. Jawaharlal Nehru, op. cit., p. 207.
77. Ibid.
78. Jawaharlal Nehru, *An Autobiography* (New Delhi: Oxford University Press, 2001), p. 13.
79. Perry Anderson, *The Indian Ideology* (Gurgaon: Three Essays Collective, 2012), p. 19.
80. Jawaharlal Nehru, op. cit., p. 15.
81. Ambedkar on Religion and Morality -17- *Shodhganga*, in https://www.google.com/search?q=The+rationalism+which+Ambedkar+adopted+was+the+rationalism+of+the+enlightenment+Th

e+principal+elements+in+it+were+%28i%29+the+concept+of-+the+scientific+method+-+the+empirical+method+supplemented+by+the+hypothetico-deductive+method+-+as+the+only+valid+method+of+human+knowledge+and+the+corollary+that+the+knowledge+yielded+by+this+method+is+the+only+valid+form+of+human+knowledge%3B+%28ii%29+the+concept+of+a+rational+morality+based+on+%28a%29+the+utilitarian+criterion+of+a+right+action+viz.+&ie=utf-8&oe=utf-8&client=firefox-b-ab

82. Hari Mohan Sharma, *Selected Speeches of Dr. B.R. Ambedkar. His Life and Philosophy* (Delhi: Signature Books International, 2013).
83. Slavoj Žižek, 'Language, Violence and Non-violence'.
84. See my *Yusuf and Zuleika. The Return of the Despot* (Delhi: Aakar Books, 2019).
85. Samir Amin, *The Liberal Virus. Permanent War and the Americanisation of the World* (Delhi: Aakar Books, 2009), pp. 7-8.
86. Ibid., pp. 11-22.

6

Caste, Dalits and the BJP's Social Engineering

Harish Wankhede

The likelihood that the Bahujan Samaj Party (BSP) will enter into political alliances with the Samajwadi Party (SP) and the Congress in Uttar Pradesh is surely giving nightmares to the Bharatiya Janata Party (BJP) regime. Political pandits understood that the SP-BSP-Congress alliance will be a formidable challenge to Hindutva politics, especially in UP, where the BJP won 71 parliamentary seats in the last general elections. Therefore, if the BJP has to repeat its 2014 performance, its strategy would be to disturb the formation of such a grand alliance. The BJP also knows that in UP, there are not many political parties with whom it can form an electoral alliance. Therefore, to challenge the political alliance between the opposition parties, it is working mainly to consolidate and expand the broad social base that had voted for the BJP in the earlier elections.

In the 2014 general elections and later in the 2017 assembly elections in UP, the BJP had devised a strategy of 'divide and rule' to counter its opposition. Within the Dalits and the OBCs, the most economically backward sections and the most socially disadvantaged groups were categorically mobilised into the Hindutva fold. For large sections within the socially deprived groups, popular collective homogeneous nomenclatures like Dalit/Bahujan/Pichda (backward) are not simply available. People often use the narrow caste categories to articulate their political claims. BJP's strategy has been to expand the caste-based social divide to suggest that one single caste should not be the sole appropriator of the power on behalf of all the collective castes. The BJP has politicised certain marginalised castes and groups and has placed them against the conventional political domination of the Yadav, Jatav and the Muslim communities.

The BJP is better in its social engineering as it has successfully alienated the dominant political actors as insignificant political opponents now. The BJP has redefined itself as an innovative party by expanding its social base into the lower OBCs and the most politically marginalised Dalit groups that are often counted as insignificant in the conventional political calculations of the SP and the BSP. The BJP has engineered caste factions within the collective traditional vote of the SP and the BSP and its shift has improved the BJP's vote share from 15 per cent in 2012 to 42 per cent in the 2017 assembly elections. It appears that the BJP is confident of retaining its social base in the upcoming elections too and therefore, the political alliance of the opposition appears a somewhat weak here.

BJP's Caste Politics

The BJP achieved such an impressive social alliance by adopting three different political strategies: First, the BJP understands that the caste system is still operative and different caste groups do not have social alliances or fraternal relationships. Castes still function with distrust, animosity and jealousy towards each other and there is no reformist force that can challenge such caste divisions. Modern democracy further allows the resurrections of social segments and factions to make distinct political claims. The BJP showed no interest in reforming the caste fragments; instead it encourages and politicises caste division so that no political collective, such as the Dalits or the OBC, can be formed. It understands that any such formation may challenge the domination of the social elites.

Therefore, aiding and promoting those caste groups that are willing to disturb the collective identity of the Dalits and the OBCs has become a prime strategy. Among the Dalits, the BJP is eyeing mainly to promote the Rajbhar, Pasi, Dhobi and Khatik castes as a counter block against the Jatav leadership of the BSP. Within the OBCs, the BJP has prioritised the Mauryas, Kurmis and Lodhs as the leading flag bearers of Hindutva politics. The SP, thus, will be restricted as a Yadav-dominated Party. The everyday social differences between caste groups are consciously manipulated to convert it into stiff social and political rivalries.

Second, there are various political announcements and policy-level promises by the BJP to keep the caste tussle alive. For example, the state government has shown a keen interest in the bifurcation of the reservation policy. It helps the party to popularise that the Yadavs, Jatavs and some other castes have monopolised most of the benefits of the reservation policy and therefore, it is time to reform the policy so that the benefits can also reach the most-backward castes. Such agenda cunningly portrays certain Dalit and OBC castes as the new middle class or dominant castes and place the other marginalised groups against them. It fosters distrust and enmity within the same social base and allows the upper caste elites to retain its domination over major economic and political resources.

Third, the BJP communalises certain cultural-folk entitlements attached to social and religious beliefs of the lower castes. Large sections of the Dalit-OBCs are still attached to the Hindu religious traditions and overwhelmingly participate in various local rituals and folklore. The RSS-BJP has systematically intervened in the cultural spheres and often manipulated these local traditions to raise communal clashes against the Muslims. The local deities, folk heroes, village traditions and other cultural artifacts are manoeuvred systematically to build a bond with the Hindutva's politics. Further, the BJP builds the anti-Muslim hatred by communalising socially sensitive issues like cow protection, Ram Temple and of 'protecting the dignity of Hindu women' against the Muslim aggressor (love jihad). The everyday intervention of the RSS-BJP in the religious and cultural milieu of the lower castes has helped the party to gain its support.

Addressing the Dalit Question

Dalit identity is a powerful political block. Its legacy of struggles for social justice has gained an iconic presence in contemporary democracy. The Ambedkarite Dalits, especially in Uttar Pradesh and Maharashtra, have resisted the Brahmanical cultural assimilation by asserting their socio-religious and political autonomy. Dalit identity has remained a bête noire to the Hindutva project and in the past, the right wing has avoided an open engagement with the caste question. The RSS-BJP combine assumes that the Dalits are an integral part of the communal Hindu identity, especially when it mobilises against the Muslims. By popularising the Brahmanical culture and religious artefacts as national symbols, the right wing attracts the Dalits into its fold.

However, against the efforts of the right wing, the Ambedkarite Dalits' stiff ideological commitment, street militancy for social justice and the religious and cultural separateness have promoted them as an arch ideological counter to right wing politics. The recent nation-wide mobilisation of Dalits against the dilution of the Scheduled Castes and Tribes (Prevention of Atrocities) Act highlights their growing anger against the political establishment.

The Rashtriya Swayamsevak Sangh (RSS) understands the dynamic legacy of the Dalit movement in disturbing the Hindutva's ideological rigour. Hence, to neutralise the impact of Dalit assertion on the political and social fronts, the right wing forces have improvised their tactics at both levels. On the political front, the BJP is showcasing its inclusive character; however, in the social sphere, the right wing is using anti-Dalit sentiments to consolidate its political base.

The Bharatiya Janata Party (BJP) promotes itself as a party committed to social justice and has highlighted that "no other government has honuored Ambedkar more than the current regime". Prime Minister Narendra Modi, who referred to himself as a 'Bhakt of Ambedkar' has also announced two grand memorials of Ambedkar at Mumbai and New Delhi. Further, the Maharashtra state government acquired the 'Ambedkar London House' by paying Rs. 40 crore, which will now become an International

Research Centre on Ambedkar. To attract Dalits, the BJP in its political campaigns has systematically used Ambedkar's name and photographs and has often promised not to disturb the reservation policy.

Last year, the election of Ramnath Kovind as the President of India was used by the BJP to showcase that the party was keen on inclusion of Dalits in its political agenda. Along with this, the BJP also showcased the importance of Dalit leaders like Ramvilas Paswan and Ramdas Athawale in running the current government. The representation of influential Dalit castes and recognition of its social symbols has become imperative in the BJP's new social engineering.

Such strategies of inclusion have surely helped the BJP improve its conventional anti-Dalit image. It has improvised its conservative 'Brahmin-Bania' party image by offering the party a liberal political character. Importantly, the RSS also understands that broader resonance of Dalit identity and its ideological merit only complicates the Hindutva's political project. The BJP also understands that such symbolic political actions and ceremonial events may attract the mobile urban Dalits but may create anxieties within its core social base. Its conventional vote bank is not the Dalits, but mainly the small town urban middle classes and the conservative upper caste population.

At the ground level, the BJP's conventional voters and Dalits have no fraternal association or social alliance. In contrast, the everyday social relationships are dominated by the cultural values of the social elites. The recent incident in Gujarat, where a young Dalit boy Pradeep Rathod was killed by the upper castes for reportedly owning and riding a horse, showcases the deep-seated hatred against Dalit assertion. Dalits face the worst kind of social prejudices, humiliation and violence against which right wing politics has no reformist agenda.

A recent study by the University of Pennsylvania under Social Attitude Research for India highlights that large sections within the upper-middle class society still hold explicit prejudices against the Dalits. Brahmanical conservatism grips the social psyche even in times of high-modernity and refuses to change. Social relationships are still disciplined through caste and communal prejudices. Muslims and Dalits face humiliation and violence every day because of the ingrained hatred constructed by the conservative Brahmanical social values. The agenda of social reform, therefore, remains incomplete, as the radical transformation of social attitudes needs annihilation of caste pride. The social elites have not only resisted the agenda of social reforms, but have also categorically treated those who stood against Brahmanical values, rituals and customs as anti-social. The claims for constitutional safeguards, reservation policy and social dignity by the Dalits are often belittled as demands of 'freeloaders' and 'non-meritorious' people.

In fact, the right wing categorically exploits the entrenched anti-Dalit social tendencies to organise its core political base. Nationalist-Hindu cultural symbols and upper caste social pride are often evoked to challenge the radical Ambedkarite demands. To satisfy its conventional conservative social base and to broaden the appeal of Hindutva, the BJP (and the RSS) apply a distinct social agenda from its political strategy.

For this government, the creation of anti-Dalit agenda began with the Rohith Vemula suicide incident. The then human resource development minister Smriti Irani went against the Dalit students' struggles in the University of Hyderabad and blamed the protesting groups for instigating caste conflicts on campus, demonstrating that Dalit protesters would henceforth be treated as ideological enemies of the government. Later, the brutal flogging of Dalits by cow vigilantes in Una in Gujarat demonstrated that Dalits would be punished with brutal violence if they disturbed the cultural conformity of Hindutva politics. Soon after, in Saharanpur, Uttar Pradesh, the popular Bhim Army leader Chandrashekhar Azad was arrested under the draconian National Security Act, mainly for organising Dalits against the exploitative hegemony of upper caste Thakurs in the region.

On the January 1, 2018, a planned attack by militant right wing groups on an annual Dalit event near Pune took place. The right wing termed the annual celebration to commemorate the Mahar soldiers' participation in the Bhima-Koregaon battle as 'anti-national' and demeaned the social history that the Dalits have created to claim their respectful position in the past. In April 2018, the Centre once again demonstrated its reluctance in the Supreme Court to protect the SC/ST Act from being diluted. It was only after massive protests by Dalit groups in all major states that the government decided to file a review petition in the court. Again, very recently, the Allahabad high court issued a guideline that is extremely detrimental to fulfilling the reservation quota in universities. Here, too, the government did not show any sensitivity to protect Dalit rights.

These are a few incidents where the ruling elites visibly went against the social aspirations and constitutional rights of Dalits. The government cared more about Hindutva's political assertion and the interests of the conservative elites. More importantly, Ambedkarite protesters are being projected as militant hate-builders against the Hindu religion and the Hindutva-led nationalist-state. On mainstream media and on various social media portals, politically conscious Dalits and their assertion for rights are being demeaned as 'narrow' appeals of a caste group and therefore harmful for the nationalist Hindutva project. There is a greater imposition of tags like miscreants, lawbreakers, Naxals and even as anti-national. Such vocabulary belittles and further alienates the Dalits. The robust collective-Hindu self is being evoked to target the 'separatist' political Dalits. These strategies on the social fronts have cunningly projected the Ambedkarite Dalits as a new social minority.

The way Muslims as the 'political other' are required to be submissive to majoritarian Hindu communalism, the Ambedkarite Dalit minority, too, is being projected as the new 'social other' to help the right wing mobilise conservative Brahmanical Hindus. One can see such trends, especially in UP and Maharashtra, where ideologically committed Dalit castes, like Jatavs and Mahars, are being projected as 'aggressive' anti-Hindutva castes. The Ambedkarite Dalits are thus branded as counter-culturists to the collective will of the Hindus and, therefore, as 'anti-social' and 'anti-national'.

In the changed political climate today, the BJP has understood the limitations of its inclusive social engineering. It is not possible for the right wing to address the issues of social justice since it goes vehemently against its own ideological mettle and disturbs its core support base. More than the politics of Dalit inclusion, the right wing has decided to return to its core Hindutva agenda. Therefore, on the ground, the BJP is trying hard to retain its conventional upper caste support. It is clear that the right wing is consciously trying to engineer a broad social alliance of upper castes and other dominant castes by projecting Ambedkarite Dalits as a new militant social 'enemy'.

Conclusion

It appears that such Machiavellian strategies had proved efficient and yielded results effectively paid the dividends to the BJP during the earlier elections and even in the upcoming elections it will be banking mostly on such strategies. However, this time, the party has very little to offer on the substantive question of social and economic justice. The material conditions of the lower OBCs and the non-Jatav Dalits have not at all improved on any indicators of human development. These groups are still socially discriminated, persecuted and surviving under precarious poverty. The BJP slogan 'Sabka Saath Sabka Vikas' has not uplifted these communities from their wretched conditions and they are still far from the corridors of power. It is only the communal and caste polarisation that has kept these communities under BJP's umbrella.

The SP-BSP-Congress alliance seems impressive on paper. The Yadav-Jatav-Muslim combination appears a winnable social engineering strategy for the opposition today. However, there is a high possibility that the RSS-BJP brigade can mobilise a bigger social collective than this. On ground, the BJP is effectively executing its own brand of caste-communal politics, against which the opposition is yet to devise any comprehensive strategy. Therefore, the task of the opposition will not be complete only by forming a political alliance.

It can become a formidable political force only if the alliance works to expand its social base and connect the other marginalised groups as equal partners. The challenges before the alliance are to work on the (negative) stereotypes associated with it and to overcome its one caste-centric character. It has to expand its social base to ensure a greater participation of other marginalised communities in the party's functioning and power structure. Simultaneously, the alliance also needs to announce a new agenda of economic welfare to challenge the rhetoric of BJP's development. An impressive ideological assertion based on the values of social justice and socialism can dismantle BJP's divisive social engineering in the upcoming elections.

Postscript

The 2019 emphatic victory of the BJP in General Elections endorsed the position that I took in this chapter. It is visible that the political strategies of social engineering that BJP invented in 2014 are still working in BJP's favour. In 2019, BJP reintroduced its formulae of social engineering and crafted a big division against the traditional votaries of social justice and secularism politics. Interestingly, it has also repackaged its brand ambassador 'the Persona of Narendra Modi' in a more aggressive manner while supplementing the whole campaign with the doses of communal nationalism. The reasons for BJP's mega victory thus have parallel and combined strategies. The face of these strategies was Modi's character and anti-Pakistan rhetoric. However at the actual ground level, a clinical understanding of caste and cultural attributes and its usage in amplifying the voice of Hindutva has made all the difference.

Region

7

North-South Divide: A study in Two Political Cultures

Rasu Chhatrapati Yadav

Electoral politics witnessed tremendous changes in seventy ycars of independent India with emergence of regional parties raking up regional identities in several states and national parties being relegated to a secondary position or forcing them to align with one regional party or the other for electoral gains and political existence. India remained under a single party rule for almost two decades after independence with the Congress winning all the elections unopposed in almost all the states, mostly due to its role in the freedom struggle while Left parties confined to principal opposition in a few states like Andhra Pradesh. However, after the initial decades of independence, regional parties emerged strongly in most of the southern states and achieved success winning the mandate of electorate and this has brought a phenomenal change in the electoral politics of the country. Kerala was the first state to have a non-Congress government with Communists winning the people's mandate and emerging victorious in 1957.

As such there is a clear evidence of the fundamental difference in electoral politics in southern and northern states with southern states dominated by regional parties and northern states ruled by non-BJP and non-Congress parties like the Janata Dal, Samajwadi Party and the Bahujan Samaj Party, which are national parties technically but were confined to certain regional pockets.

The present chapter is divided into five sections highlighting the major fundamental differences in North-South politics in the Indian federation. The first section deals with the politics dominated by the Dravidian movement influenced by the demands of the lower castes in the southern states, whereas a similar situation does not arise in North India where Brahmanical forces and politics dominated the political sphere. The second section examines the advent of regional identity and emergence of major political forces based on linguistic identity in all southern states. The third section highlights how these regional parties have become strong and a force to reckon with in South India and have raised their ante demanding more powers from the Centre as a true reflection of federalism. The fourth section discusses how the regional parties have succeeded in raking up strong anti-Congressism and anti-BJPism sentiments in southern states compared to northern states which are under the influence of either one national party or the other carried on by Hindutva forces. The fifth section focuses on the domination of family and hereditary politics with almost all the regional parties in South India are managed by the families. In North India the phenomenon has not emerged to that magnitude as has been seen in South India with the exception of the National Conference and PDP in Jammu and Kashmir.

Anti-Brahmin and Shudra Caste Dominated Politics in South India

South Indian politics is dominated by strong anti-Brahmin, Shudra and Dravidian movements which were prevalent in the erstwhile Madras Presidency including parts of Andhra Pradesh, Tamil Nadu, Karnataka and Kerala. Even during the nationalist movement, different political voices were raised in South India unlike in North India with dissonance from the dominant Congress politics in terms of demands and aspirations of the lower castes.

South Indian politics is influenced by the demands of lower castes and this has resulted in the formation of the South Indian Liberation Federation (SILF), popularly known as Justice Party in 1916 in Tamil Nadu. Prominent non-Brahmin leaders started the Justice Party which won the first legislative elections in Madras Presidency in 1920. The Justice Party along with the Self Respect Movement was later rechristened as Dravida Kazhagam (DK) under the leadership of Periyar E.V. Ramaswamy and the party remained a strong political force and a beacon of social justice.[1] Later the DK got divided into Dravida Khazagham (DK), Dravida Munnetra Kazagham (DMK) and the All India Anna Dravida Munnetra Kazagham (AIADMK).

In Andhra Pradesh, the upper Shudra castes (Reddys and Kammas) dominated political leadership right from its inception. The dominant landed elite constituting Reddys from coastal Andhra Pradesh and Rayalaseema occupied Chief Minister's posts from 1956 to the late 1970s in the Congress governments. The Congress regimes were led by socially and economically dominant castes, i.e. Brahmins and upper caste Shudras, the Reddys. The launch of regional party, Telugu Desam (TD), by actor Nandamuri Taraka Rama Rao, popularly known as NTR and its ascendancy to power within six months of its inception riding on 'Telugu Pride' has changed the dynamics of politics in Andhra Pradesh. The TD pitched Telugu sentiment and questioned the frequent change of chief ministers by Congress leadership and has succeeded in projecting it as a North Indian party. TD's entry has also changed the social composition of politics in the state with the Kammas emerging as politically powerful and NTR himself, a Kamma, introduced populist schemes like Rs.-2-a-kg rice and subsidised power and fertilisers attracting the poor and farmers into the party fold. The charisma he enjoyed among Telugu people as matinee idol for portraying mythological characters in movies has helped the party in elections. TD gave prominence to henceforth neglected communities like Backward Classes (BC) which are numerically high in the state and many of the educated BCs have been elevated as second-rung leaders making the party a formidable force among

BCs. Till then these sections have the feeling of being neglected by the Congress whose focus was mainly on Scheduled Castes and Scheduled Tribes. Reservations for Other Backward Classes (OBCs) after the Mandal Commission, successful implementation of reservations in Panchayat Raj institutions and TD's measure to introduce the three-tier Panchayat system resulting in creation of mandals has resulted in BCs emerging as leaders and helped the TD in consolidating its base among OBCs.[2] Till then panchayat samithis were dominated by dominant castes. Using these factors, the Telugu Desam expanded its social base and remained a force to reckon with till the formation of the Telangana state.

In Karnataka, the Vokkaligas and Lingayats exercised their hold over the political leadership in the state with majority of the leaders in the Congress and Janata Dal (Secular) and the Bharatiya Janata Party (BJP). While Congress and the JD (S) enjoy the support of the Vokkaligas it is the Lingayats who form the strong base for the BJP with its strong leader B.S. Yedyurappa being the face of the party in the state.

Pro-Brahmin and High Caste Dominated Politics in North India

Politics in North India is dominated by Brahminical forces. Take for example, Uttar Pradesh, Bihar, Madhya Pradesh, Maharashtra where Brahmins, Dwija community castes such as Rajputs in Madhya Pradesh and Rajasthan occupy the political leadership. In Maharashtra in spite of Mahatma Jyothirao Phuley's movement for social justice, politics in the state is dominated by Brahmins. Only from the 1970s, non-Brahmins came into prominence in the political sphere in North India with Mulayam Singh Yadav in Uttar Pradesh and Lalu Prasad Yadav in Bihar becoming the prominent leaders from the backward classes and Marathas and Patels of Marathas in Maharashtra.

The most striking feature of regional parties in North India is that they are not ideologically based but represent only certain sections and ally with regional parties only to get majority votes and win a mandate in elections and do not strive for social emancipation. In North India, upper castes consolidated their political leadership by co-opting Backward Classes and lower castes with second-rung leadership. This is termed as 'Coalition of Extremes' according to which Congress wooed Scheduled Castes and co-opted political leadership to serve its purposes and ensure domination over BCs and Dalits.[3]

Regional Identity: Domination of Regional Parties

Unlike North India, politics in South India is dominated by regional identity and regional pride like Telugu Identity, Tamil Identity, Malayali Identity and Kannada Identity. The demand for formation or division of states on linguistic lines started in South India and the Telugu-speaking people of Andhra region in the erstwhile Madras Presidency were the first who arose for this cause and launched a huge agitation for an exclusive state for Telugu-speaking people. This materialised with the formation of Andhra State, which was again merged with the Telangana region, till then in the Nizam province, to form Andhra Pradesh State in 1956. Similarly, there were movements like Aikya Karnataka Movement, Ikya Kerala Movement since parts of Kerala were in Madras Presidency. Such demands were witnessed in Karnataka too as some parts of Karnataka were in Bombay Presidency and some in Tamil Nadu.

Now a new identity has emerged after Telangana state was separated from Andhra Pradesh. Telangana Rashtra Samithi (TRS) has benefited with Telangana sentiments and capitalised on the protracted agitation undertaken by the people's organisations, students, civil society and the masses demanding separate statehood protesting the hegemony of Andhra Pradesh over the region. The TRS won the first Assembly elections in the newly formed Telangana State in 2014.

There is no regional identity in North India though a few states like Chhattisgarh, Jharkhand and Uttarakhand are formed. No regional parties emerged in these states and still national parties, the Congress, the BJP, BSP and SP dominate politics in these states. This could be attributed to the continuous domination of Brahmanical and forward castes over the political leadership and lack of initiative from the Dalit and Backward Classes to emerge as an alternative leadership. Though the Bahujan Samaj Party and Samajwadi Party ruled the Uttar Pradesh state twice once in coalition and then alone, they lost the opportunity in consolidating the electorates belonging to Dalits, Backward Classes and Minorities in making it a vote bank on which they could bank upon in future.

The major shift which has happened in North India is the shift in the vote bank of tribals from the Congress to the BJP. The tribals who stood rock solid behind the Congress have started supporting the BJP and the most surprising aspect is the emergence of the BJP as a strong political force in the tribal-dominated state of Chhattisgarh. The factors which helped this was the systematic and prolonged strategy adopted by Hindutva forces Rashtriya Swayamsevak Sangh (RSS) and its affiliate Vanvasi Kalyan Ashrams (VKA) which run health camps in tribal hamlets, mobilising tribals and also distinguishing them from tribals who got converted to Christainity. The successful polarisation of Hindu and Christian the tribals has helped the BJP in consolidating the tribal vote bank, especially Gonds whose population is numerically higher compared to other tribals[4]. These efforts have helped the BJP emerging victorious for three consecutive terms in 2003, 2008 and 2013.

Linguistic Identity and Politics of Language: National Parties with Regional Colours

With the demand for states on linguistic basis, politics in South India is largely dominated by regional parties. Even national parties like the Communist Party of India (Marxist) functions or acts as a regional party in Kerala and there is no relationship between the CPI (M) of Kerala and CPI (M) of West Bengal and elsewhere. One can conclude that CPI (M) acts as a Malayali party as it was active in the linguistic movement and has a Malayalam identity. Similarly, Tamil Nadu witnessed Tamil nationalism and the Dravidian movement and in Andhra Pradesh also the concept of 'Telugu pride' raked up by the Telugu Desam has become a success among the electorate.

Most of the regional parties have been strengthened by taking up the language as a major symbol of assertion and opposing national parties, the Congress in the early years of independence and later BJP in the recent past. Southern States, Tamil Nadu, Andhra Pradesh, Karnataka and Kerala stand as a testimony to these efforts. DMK and the AIADMK have been successful in evoking the Tamil sentiment as they strongly opposed the imposition of Hindi and the idea of nationalism propagated by the national parties. Karunanidhi of DMK established memorials, monuments and idols of Tamil kings as the cultural symbols of Tamil country, countering the anti-Hindi and anti-North influence ensuring that Dravidian politics are different from the mainstream nationalism[5]

Anti-Congressism and Anti-BJPism in South India

South Indian politics has an element of anti-Congressism and anti-BJPism because South India politics is dominated by Shudra castes. In all southern states, while Reddys and Kammas dominated political leadership and emerged as the political class in the state of Andhra Pradesh, Velamas, another upper caste Shudra emerged as a political force in Telangana state. The basic premise on which Telugu Desam was formed is on the Telugu pride and against autocratic functioning of Congress by changing chief ministers without giving any audience to state leaders. In Karnataka though the Congress remained in power, Janata Dal emerged strong.

BJP's Hindutva is seen as Brahmanical so South India politics could be termed as Shudra caste politics dominated by Shudra upper castes. Therefore, it is difficult for Hindutva votaries to establish dominance in South India. Hindutva could dominate in areas where it could co-opt Shivism as in Karnataka, i.e. Shivist Hindutva.

This strong communal bonding reflected by syncretism for which Karnataka is popularly known with several shrines standing as a testimony to the flourishing Hindu-Muslim unity has been breached and Hindutva forces made several attempts to occupy political and social space by appropriating cultural symbols, syncretic culture and Hindu festivals, especially in the coastal Karnataka.[6]

Karnataka witnessed several communal riots in the recent past in Mangalore, Udipi, Tumkur, Kolar, Bemgaum and symbols of syncretism like Baba Budan Giri experienced communal politics appropriating secular spaces and the state has become a place for competitive communalism and reactive communalism[7]. The national parties have a strong counter point in regional party formation.

Regional Parties: Anti-Centric and Federal Structure

Based on the above premises, electoral politics, regional identity, regional specificity becomes important as a social-cultural aspect of politics. As an organisational aspect most of the regional parties in South India are anti-Centre, i.e. Dravidian parties like Dravida Kazhagam, DMK, AIADMK and Telugu Desam.

Regional parties articulated an anti-Centre policy for more decentralised power distribution and for a balanced Centre-State relationships. Telugu Desam was in the forefront in articulating the state powers and federalism within the state and Centre's powers and the controversial role of the Governor. The dismissal of N.T. Rama Rao and reinstatement of his junior as chief minister in his absence for his strong anti-Congress stand and the dismissal of the S.R. Bommai government of Janata Dal had helped in forging a strong alliance between regional parties against the Congress at the Centre and the party was instrumental in forming a coalition government at the Centre in 1989. Telugu Desam was vocal in advocating the need to protect the federal structure and interests of the regional parties. Janata Dal (Secular) in Karnataka, TD, AIADMK and DMK have a common agenda of regionalism with more powers for the state and are instrumental in coming together to form the third front government at the Centre.

Therefore, South Indian politics is different from North Indian politics. There is a clear decline of the Congress in South India and difficulty for the expansion of the Bharatiya Janata Party, in spite of several attempts.

Hereditary and Family Politics

Hereditary and family politics is the hallmark of the regional parties in South India and to some extent in North India as well. Most of the regional parties are family parties with one family having full control over the functioning of the party, i.e. DMK,

Telugu Desam, Yuvajana Shramika Raithu Congress (YSRC), JD (S) and the TRS with the presidents of these parties emerging as local satraps. North India is no exception to this phenomenon as has been seen in the Samajwadi Party in Uttar Pradesh, RJD in Bihar and National Conference and PDP in Jammu and Kashmir.

Andhra Pradesh and Telangana: Polarisation on Caste Lines

The Chandrababu Naidu government during the early 1990s played a crucial role in raking up the controversial issue of categorisation of Scheduled Castes based on the demand of Madigas that reservations within SCs are being usurped by Malas depriving them of their share in education and employment. It is a known fact that Scheduled Castes remained a strong vote bank of the Congress since independence and with this move, Naidu has been successful in ensuring that SC votes remain divided between two parties, the TD and the Congress with the majority of Madigas supporting the TD for championing for SC categorisation while Malas supporting the Congress. Also SCs were divided on regional lines with Madigas being numerically strong in Telangana while Malas are in large numbers in Andhra. In this dominant discourse, the issues of numerically weak SC castes lost their relevance with no party addressing their problems.

The demand by the numerically strong dominant caste Kapus for reservations in coastal Andhra was exploited by parties with successive governments assuring to fulfil their promise though it has to overcome the constitutional bottlenecks as the Supreme Court imposed a ceiling in providing reservations to the socially backward communities, up to 50 per cent.

Kapus, Telaga, Balija and Ontari communities which are numerically strong with 27 per cent in Andhra remained the vote bank of the Congress and to groom them Naidu has promised them reservation in education and jobs but failed to honour it except for constituting a committee and allocating five per cent quota which is likely to increase the reservation percentage to more than 50 per cent ceiling imposed by the Supreme Court.

In the Assembly elections held in the state of Telangana in December 2018, with a slew of welfare programmes catering to different communities, especially farmers and several BC-centric programmes like distribution of sheep, buffaloes to Yadavs, fish seedlings for Mudhiraj (fishermen), dhobi ghats for washermen, and barber shops, the ruling Telangana Rashtra Samithi romped home to power for the consecutive second term.

TRS targeted elderly people by extending Rs. 1,000 a month pension and wooed Muslims, EBCs, BCs, SCs, STs with Kalayana Lakshmi and Shaadi Mubarak programmes (financial assistance of Rs. 1 lakh for performing the marriage of girl child) with a whopping Rs. 1,700 crores benefiting nearly three lakh girls.[8]

The TRS doled out many schemes to attract several occupational castes and even forward castes. The Crop Investment Scheme, popularly known as Rythu Bandhu scheme meant to provide Rs. 8,000 an acre a year as investment to raise crops without any upper ceiling is meant to woo small and marginal farmers and landlords, especially the Reddys who owned large tracts of lands with the majority being absentee farmers. Apart from these sections, the scheme also benefited many BCs and SCs who own small and marginal farm landholdings.

The TRS government has agreed to provide 12 per cent reservation for Muslims and increase the reservations for STs from the existing 6 to 10 per cent. All these will surely face legal bottlenecks but the governments are least bothered as they want to keep these communities in good humour and enjoy their patronage for their electoral gains.

The Jana Sena of actor Pawan Kalyan, who belongs to the Kapu community is pinning his hopes on his community votes while Y.S. Jagan Mohan Reddy's YSRC is trying to woo the Reddys, Dalits, Christian Dalits and Kapus. To counter these parties, Naidu accommodated many Kapu leaders into the cabinet giving them important portfolios to ensure the support of the community.

In the recent Assembly elections in Telangana, the BJP tried to polarise electorates on communal lines by focusing on those areas where Muslim electorates are in a sizeable number. For example, in Karimnagar, Hyderabad and other places, several top BJP leaders including its national president Amit Shah, Prime Minister

Narendra Modi, Chief Minister of Uttar Pradesh Yogi Adityanath, Union Ministers and several RSS activists campaigned for the BJP candidate who stood second and Congress at third position. However, the BJP failed miserably and secured the lone Assembly seat with seven per cent vote share. The TRS emerged victorious and this was made possible with Muslims choosing the TRS instead of traditional Congress fearing victory of the BJP candidate.

Certain facts need to be analysed to know the voting behaviour of electorates community-wise and region-wise in these elections,. It was found that most of Adivasis who live in forests voted for Prajakutami (people's alliance of the Congress, TD, TJS and the CPI) and not for TRS and this was attributed to selective patronage of Lambadas and plain tribals by the TRS. Adivasis allege that the Lambadas were usurping most of the reservation benefits. Treatment meted out by the TRS to Adivasis prevented them from taking up podu cultivation. The TRS was also adept in giving priority to Malas within SCs who are numerically in second position to Madigas in the state.

The TRS has succeeded in eroding the base of the Telugu Desam by attracting the BCs into its fold. Ministerial berths were allocated to important BC leaders belonging to Munnuru Kapus, Yadavs, Gouds and Mudiraj. Several programmes were launched for these sections with much visibility. Even forward caste sections were also taken care of by promising financial assistance to build caste bhavans and hostels and increasing the honorarium to priests and imams.

In Tamil Nadu, the two Dravidian parties, DMK and AIADMK enjoyed people's mandate with the support of numerically strong OBCs and dominant castes and there was no scope for the Congress which lost ground in the 1960s. In Karnataka, the Lingayats and Vokkaligas dominate the political leadership irrespective of the party in power.

Left Movements and Influence of Left Parties in South India

Left parties have tremendous influence on political character of southern states, especially in Kerala where CPM was in power on several occasions and is considered as the last citadel of the Left bastion in India. The policies of the Leftist movement have influence on electorates and remain a check to the expansion of religious and bigotry politics of the BJP. The Left parties were the major opposition in Andhra Pradesh till the advent of the Telugu Desam. The erstwhile Andhra Pradesh witnessed violent Left movements like Telangana Peasants Armed Struggle from 1946-51 and extreme Left parties like CPI (ML) People's War and several ML factions have influence on electorates. The presence of the Left parties and their policies have acted as a check to the expansion of Hindutva forces and helped in protecting the secular fabric of society in Andhra Pradesh and Telangana states. In a major shift from the central leadership, the local unit of CPI (M) of Telangana state has taken up caste as an issue making a major shift in its ideology of identifying only class and formed an electoral alliance (Bahujan Left Front) with like-minded parties under Lal-Neel (Left and Bahujan) concept and contested in the recently held Telangana Assembly elections, but fared poorly losing deposits in almost all the seats.

Conclusion

There is a fundamental difference in electoral politics of North and South India. While regional parties have a major say without the involvement of national parties, especially the BJP and the Congress, the state parties, are region-specific, unlike northern parties, fighting for the interests of the states, and has a strong presence in protecting regional identity. Secondly, lower castes, Dalits and Backward Classes have a say in regional parties with ruling parties accommodating them in the decision-making process thereby giving them a sense of belongingness. Third, it is the absence of communal bent among regional parties which are more secular giving enough space for religious communities in political positions.

Southern States witnessed the Left movements. South India has largely remained a tolerant society for a long time even in the times of pre and post-independent India as no major communal riots have been reported in any part of the southern states except for a few pockets in the erstwhile princely state of the Nizam of

Hyderabad. However things have changed dramatically with the post-Ayodhya phenomenon and the expansion of Hindutva forces.

Gujarat has remained the laboratory for the Hindutva forces to experiment in the direction of the Hindu state. Ayodhya and the Ram Janmabhoomi issue has raked up the communal clashes in Northern India camouflaging the secular credentials of several parties and also the secular spaces available in the political spheres. Apart from Advani's Ratha Yatra, Gujarat has witnessed several rath yatras by the Hindutva forces reinforcing the educated middle classes and upper castes towards the Hindutva ideology and also to align with the BJP. The impact of the ratha yatras which has spread from Gujarat to Uttar Pradesh enveloping the entire Hindi belt has transformed the way people started looking at religion.

Regional parties have succeeded to a larger extent in gaining the confidence of the minorities, especially the Muslims with their liberal and secular credentials rather than anti-Muslim rhetoric adopted by the BJP and other Hindutva parties. However, this was not the case in Maharashtra, where the Shiv Sena which was formed on the slogans of Hindutva as an ideological and political slogan has succeeded to a greater extent in polarising the society on communal lines. In this way regional parties in southern states are more balanced when it comes to politics and in encouraging the liberal political thoughts and have clearly demarcated religion from politics though they have successfully included the caste aspect.

Presently Kerala has become a laboratory for Hindutva forces and controversy has been raked up on allowing women of all ages into the Sabarimala temple to polarise the electorate on communal lines in Kerala. Though the Supreme Court has given a ruling in favour of entry of women of all ages into the temple, protests and counter protests were launched to give a communal angle and exploit the situation to polarise the society. No party is in a position to antagonise any community as they remained silent on the issue.

Discourse during elections also differs in the North and South India, with majority of the discourses in South India confining to developmental and welfare issues with no scope for religious or communal politics. Also, high literacy rate and education and priority to development indexes like health, livelihood and employment give no scope for Hindutva forces in South India.

Postscript

The 2019 general election results reaffirm and reiterate the domination of the regional parties and a strong anti-BJP sentiment in South India. Though the entire North India was carried away by the Hindutva rhetoric and divisive narrative, except for Karnataka, all South Indian states have completely rejected the polarisation politics adopted by the BJP. Dravidian parties are effective in stopping Hindutva forces in Tamil Nadu with their strong regional, linguistic aspirations and identities and pluralistic ideologies. Kerala remained the most liberal thinking and progressive society showing an exemplary example on how to tackle religious chauvinism and attempts to polarise electorates (i.e. Sabarimala temple entry controversy) on religious lines with voters completely rejecting polarisation attempts and aggressive campaign of the Hindutva forces and also of the ruling Left's response. The only aberration to successful stoppage of BJP domination in South India is Telangana state where the BJP could gain substantially at the cost of the Congress and absence of any other regional party. The present elections throw huge challenges to regional parties as far as South India is concerned. The BJP's success in Karnataka could be due to the complete failure of regional parties in that state and the fissures within the alliance government while in Telangana the absence of regional forces and weak Congress helped BJP occupy the political space.

Overall the general election results have thrown a huge challenge to regional parties in South India known for their pluralistic character; how successful will they emerge in coming years depends on how effective they would be in protecting the regional, pluralistic and liberal identities in the face of increased onslaught of the Hindutva forces and polarisation politics.

References

Muralidharan, K. (2016, November 20). *100 Years of Justice Party, a Movement which Defined Tamil Nadu Politics*. Retrieved January 10, 2019, from thenewsminute.com: https://www.thenewsminute.com/article/100-years-justice-party-movement-which-defined-tamil-nadu-politics-53163

Srinivasulu, K. (2017). Region, Caste and Politics in Andhra Pradesh: Mapping the Paradigm Shift in the State Politics. In H. Roy, M.P. Singh, and A.P.S. Chouhan (eds.), *State Politics in India* (pp. 34-55). New Delhi: Primus Books.

Brass, P. (1980). The Politicisation of the Peasantry in a North India State. *Journal of Peasant Studies*, *8* (1), 3-36.

Raghuraman, S. (March 16, 2004). How BJP Won Over Tribals. *The Times of India*, p. 6.

Ramajayam, P. (2017). Dravidian State Politics: From Social Reform to Populism. In H. Roy, M.P. Singh, and A.P.S. Chouhan (eds.), *State Politics in India* (pp. 727-758). New Delhi: Primus Books.

Assadi, M. (2002). Hindutva Policies in Coastal Region: Towards a Social Coalition. *Economic and Political Weekly, 28* (23), 2211-13.

Assadi, M. (2009). Competitive Communalism: and Reactive Communalism, Recent Communal Riots in Mysore. *Indian Journal of Secularism, 13* (3), 25-33.

https://cgg.gov.in/it_project/kalyana-lakshmi-shaadi-mubarak/

Media

8

The Political Economy of Elections and Media in Contemporary Times

Noorjahan Momin

Traditionally the means of informing and educating people, media's role has undergone a drastic change in the era of globalisation. What was known as the 'fourth pillar of a democracy' has successfully metamorphosed itself into a big business with immense potential of turning into an oligarchic force and has been used as a tool for the convergence of interests of the political and economic elites. The closeness between echelons of media and corridors of governmental power has granted this medium of communication with significant power. In his seminal work *Taking the Risk Out of Democracy: Corporate Propaganda versus Freedom and Liberty*, Alex Carey writes: 'The twentieth century has been characterised by three developments of great political importance: the growth of democracy, the growth of corporate power and the growth of corporate propaganda as a means of protecting corporate power against democracy' (Carey, 1997). This chapter looks at Carey's assertion with special reference to the evolved role of media in the most important aspect of democracy, i.e. elections. An attempt is also made at understanding this transition with special reference to the Indian case.

The Transformation

The manner, in which media has been actively involved in the making and breaking of electoral fortunes of those who embody the capability to influence it, is no misnomer today. The active participation of media in the Indian election campaign of the last general election in 2014, is not the sole example of this change in the transformation of the role of media. Even after the elections were concluded with a thumping majority for the Bharatiya Janata Party, this tendency has further strengthened rather than subsiding. The news–about day-to-day lives, issues and struggles; inefficiency of the government and the ever degrading state of the Indian economy– has been pushed beyond the periphery of general conscience and knowledge. What has come to the centre stage is an overt propaganda that is designed and smartly packaged to benefit the political party or parties that may work towards strengthening the economic prospects, in the long run, of the capitalists who control media.

However, the situation has not always been so bleak. Media emerged as a mode of communication, information and interest articulation. The role mass media played during the French Revolution is a shining example of the same. So was the case of the role of newspapers and magazines during the anti-colonial movement in the Third World countries, whereby it performed the task of nation-building revolving around a cultivated sense of a common identity, helped in interest articulation and channelised the public discontent and unrest against the colonial rulers to form a unified and structured movement of independence (Desai 1948 (1959). *Iskra*, the political newspaper brought out by the Russian Socialist Democratic Labour Party is another such example. On the contrary, there are also examples where the media has had a symbiotic relationship with the state, whereby it aligned itself with the all-pervasive strength of the state. The South African media provided justifications, thus legitimising the discriminatory policy of apartheid.

The Wind of Change

The role of media underwent drastic transformation by the beginning of the last decade of the twentieth century. With the efforts of bringing the world economy at large, and the Third World economies in particular under the same centralised regime, massive reforms were brought about that unleashed the force of liberalisation, globalisation and privatisation. Mass media too crumbled under this pressure. The transition was not superficial and limited to the nature of coverage and texture of news. This was a far deeper running change that had its genesis in the change in the ownership and management structure of these institutions.

India was no exception to this trajectory of 'development'. It too adopted the system of liberalisation which pivoted around privatisation of economic resources. An aspect of this transformation was the loot of state assets during the initial phase of privatisation. While the state's role receded in the background, at mass level capitalists were vehemently acquiring state-owned enterprises or entered into joint ownership through overt or covert acquisition. On the pretext of providing financial aid to the Third World countries the World Bank and IMF imposed necessary conditions of economic reforms. The loans and financial aid under these reforms were given with the illusion of providing an impetus to the stagnating economy; however, their actual objective included transformation of the socialist or socialist-like economies into market economies as well as integrating them into the global financial system. These states were compelled to accept these demands from the prevalent hegemonic financial system.

Surrendering to these demands meant the opening of floodgates for private players in various sectors as well as incorporation of newer sectors in the category of business. Opening up these sectors to private investment led to influx of foreign investment in these sectors. The scope and importance of this sector was further accentuated due to the recently occurred information and telecommunication revolution. While oil, transportation, manufacture were well-known sectors; a new sector was emerging as a potentially lucrative business for private players. While on the superficial level the state's role was changing, at a deeper level what was transpiring was the emergence of a strong lobby of private economic players. Many of these players had always been present in these societies; but they were still under the control of the state. The difference now was that rather than the state calling the shots, it was these private economic players who were arm-twisting the state into submission. To camouflage this overhaul a new sector was fast emerging.

This sector was media business. Speaking about this new sector that gained tremendous importance in the age of privatisation, Prof. Deepak Kumar says: "In Nehru's time, the communication ministry was hardly lucrative. From the 1990s onwards, thanks to the rapid technological changes, influential politicians have bargained for this ministry. Two of the union communication ministers have graced the jail and the third rests in heaven" (Kumar 2016). The economic liberalisation brought a surge of foreign investment and 'corporatisation', but not without a cost.

The "unmanageable" strong and independent editors were considered 'undesirable' by the central and state governments, as well as the opposition parties. Now, the major editorial decisions were taken not at the editorial boards' meeting; but rather by the management boards of media houses. This all pervasive interference–from the kind of news to be reported to the hiring of journalists (Khare 2018)–made the marketing director more significant in the newsrooms than the editor. Editors, who were known for their intellect, experience, skill, grit and courage to not buckle down before the governmental pressure, were shown the door. Those who still persisted or took charge of the situation through their independent endeavours were exterminated. The killing of Gauri Lankesh and the prevailing impunity expressed by the conspirators, perpetrators, and propagator of this hateful crimes reeks of the rot in the system. In the United States of America the former executive editor of the *Times*, Jill Abramson, attributes her resistance to more communication between the business and editorial sides of the newspaper, which according to the internal "innovation report" were necessary for the success of the publication in this digital age, as one of the reasons for her sacking (Abramson 2019).

In a country where the very first case in India pertaining to freedom of expression as a fundamental right was also filed by two print publications; this downward spinning is worrying. For their interventions and knack for taking a stand, media has also reported the maximum casualties not just in terms of loss of employment, but rather in more serious punitive repercussions such as assassinations, censorship, banning and arrests of journalists and editors at the behest of the ruling regime. In 2017 alone as many as 11 journalists were killed, 46 were attacked, and 27 cases of police action such as detention, arrests were being filed, and 12 cases of threats were reported against journalists in India (*The India Freedom Report 2017*). However, things are taking a southward dip in recent times in a very different manner.

Even when one cites the shining examples of resistance and street-fighting spirit of some members of the media fraternity in India and globally even today, one cannot help noticing the sporadic nature of these examples. What has taken place of the legendary courageous journalism is media-savvy, governmental rewards seeking, PR agents like journalists.

From Media to Media Business: The Political Economy of Change

In the last twenty-five years, media and the communication sector has transformed itself into a major business entity, resembling any other business struggling to maintain its foothold while trying to grow simultaneously with the passing of each financial year in a liberal economy. The collateral in this transformation was that the media lost its distinction as the fourth pillar of a thriving democracy that aspired to bring accountability in the government. What emerged instead was a business that was constantly seeking to work on a give and take norm with the government to secure its economic fortunes. Another important aspect of this metamorphosis of the media was that those industrialists and capitalists who had so far remained completely aloof from the avenue of news reporting and broadcasting were now acquiring ownership rights over media enterprises.

In contemporary India, companies belonging to industrial magnates Mukesh Ambani and Gautam Adani hold ownership rights of several television channels. When the Indian economy was initially opened for privatisation, we witnessed the emergence of private news channels in India; and with this emerged a new economic sector. With the introduction of foreign capital in the Indian economy, a different phenomenon began taking shape in the Indian media sector as well. Rupert Murdoch-owned Star Network invested in India through a contract with NDTV. This was one of the largest investments of those times (Kaushik 2015). On similar lines, other non-governmental channels Zee News and Aaj Tak also emerged as major players on the Indian media horizon. The fact that they were voices other than the so-called governmental mouthpiece Doordarshan, gave a boost to their image as independent sources of information. However, it must be reiterated here that the role private capital played for creating opinion in favour or against the government became obvious only in recent times.

Even in the Russian case the closeness between the media and the government is not a hidden fact. This dovetailing between the state machinery and private business enterprises became evident during Yeltsin's second attempt at the presidential election in 1996, when his bid for re-election coincided with the rising discontent against his policies and state of Russian economy. The dream of economic progress that was sold during the disintegration period was exposed as a mere chimera. This added fuel to the fire of dissatisfaction against him. In the wake of people's disillusionment, erosion of people's life savings and incremental rise in hardship, Yeltsin's popularity was rapidly declining. In the Duma elections of December 1995 the emergence of the Communist Party of Russia as the largest party was an alarming situation for the pro-liberalisation and privatisation lobby. The Liberal Democratic Party of Russia gained the second position, whereas Yeltsin's Our Home is Russia Party secured a mere two per cent of votes. Boris Yeltsin and capitalists perceived these electoral results as a threat to the re-emergence of the Soviet legacy and socialist economic system, which would seriously jeopardise their economic and political interests.

In these circumstances, Yeltsin sought the help of the prominent capitalists for his electoral campaign. Reacting upon his call, the media companies played an extensive role in creating a positive image of him. According to Yeltsin's claim, the capitalists had offered help in his electoral campaign because that was the only means of saving their economic interests. Describing this phenomenon, Gill asserted that the business elite and the oligarchs became active in support of President Yeltsin when his ouster became an imminent threat to their personal economic interests (Gill 1998). With the objective of securing their newly gained economic freedom from being swept away by resurgence of the communists, the business elite organised itself in Yeltsin's support. This campaign for Yeltsin bears a strong similarity with the manner in which the electoral campaign was designed and implemented in India for the 2014 parliamentary elections. In both these elections, capitalists pumped in money and other resources as a means of investments that would in the long run ensure the maintenance of status quo and thus preserve their interests. In this quest for preservation, they eventually became active to such a large extent in the Russian political realm that they gained the reputation of being 'the third government' (Goldman 2003).

To counter the rising support for the communist party, a nationalist and communist image of Yeltsin was very carefully created under this strategy. People who were in the forefront in this quest of creating a positive image of Boris Yeltsin included owners of major media companies. ORT Channel One's Chairman Boris Berezovsky, NTV's CEO Igor Maleshenkov and NTV Channel 4's Vladimir Guisinky were some of the prominent people who took charge of not just leading Yeltsin's electoral campaign and image building but also managing the funds of his electoral campaign (Hoffman 2002). This carefully drawn strategy involved a positive coverage for the incumbent president in such a manner that it would transform into maximum gains in the electoral foray. Thus is could be said that image creation or rather manipulation for benefits in elections that was done in the 2014 elections was neither the first of its kind nor an isolated incident. Collaboration with the media houses has been used by leaders from across the world. The way even Hitler's fascist regime used the support of industrialists to strengthen his regime is another example of this nexus between the political and economic elite to secure the interests of both these strata of society. This trend continued even during the presidency of Vladimir Putin (Chenoy and Kumar 2017).

It has been mentioned earlier in the course of this chapter that even APCO Worldwide has designed a similarly positive image building exercise to boost the electoral gains of the present prime minister of India. His speeches were broadcasted live through all the major television channels. News and feature content represented him as the '*Vikas Purush*' (Man for Development). The coverage by several news channels such as Zee News and Times Now was lopsided to such an extent that these channels were accused of following the agenda of the BJP rather than informing their viewers about the true events and issues. In return, the owner of Zee News, Subhash Chandra was sent to the Upper House (Rajya Sabha) of the Indian parliament by the BJP. One rather interesting point worth mentioning here is that the Bharatiya Janata Party's claims to fight the menace of black money and has carried out an elaborate and rather misadventurous exercise of Demonetisation to curb the menace of Black Money and its member of parliament, Chandra's name appeared in recently published Paradise Papers–a list of those who had evaded taxation by hoarding their money in offshore entities (*The Indian Express*, 2017).

Both Yeltsin and Modi received a conspicuous amount of positive coverage for their electoral campaign and the role played by public relations managers cannot be overlooked. In both cases, media projected these politicians as strong leaders and men of great character devoid of any traces of corruption. This elaborate image-building exercise was conducted while sidelining the opposition by either not giving them enough broadcast space or by maligning the image of their leaders by caricaturing them and calling them immature and incompetent at running the polity. In Russia, the joint candidate of the unified opposition against Yeltsin was Gennady Zyuganov (of the Communist Party of the Russian Federation), received minimal broadcast space. Despite being a strong contender against Yeltsin, Zyuganov could not gather support–monetary and otherwise–from the media groups. Whatever coverage he received was in newspapers such as *Sovetskaya Rossiya*, *Pravada* and *Zavtra* which were not supporting the candidature of Boris Yeltsin (McFaul 1997). Similarly, in India opposition leaders Sonia Gandhi, Rahul Gandhi, Arvind Kejriwal, Lalu Prasad Yadav, Mamata Banerjee and Sitaram Yechury received comparatively minimal coverage. The caricaturing of leaders other than those belonging to the BJP have been evident in India since 2013.

Ensuring Yeltsin's victory in the presidential elections, the capitalists transformed themselves into oligarchs. This transformation was a symptom of the rapidly growing crony capitalism in Russia. Boris Berezovsky, Vladimir Gusinsky, Mikhail Fridman, Alexander Smolensky, Vladimir Potanin, Mikhail Khodorkovsky, and Vladimir Vinogradov who primarily controlled media, the banking sector, oil, gas, minerals and metal businesses rapidly transformed themselves from capitalists to oligarchs by wielding substantial force in the power corridors. After his re-election, Yeltsin appointed these capitalists at several prominent posts in the government. He further granted them innumerable benefits, thus boosting their economic interests. For example, Gusinsky's NTV's minority shares were bought by the state company and by a presidential order his channel received 24 hour broadcast permission (Hoffman 2002). In India also, the way several business groups owned by a few capitalists have been receiving generous doles in the form of contracts and subsidies are not a hidden fact (Thakurta et al. 2017; *Business Standard* 2016; Bahree 2014; Nair 2017).

Conclusion

The economic policies of the last decade of the twentieth century and the overhaul of the socio-economic and political system across the world has transformed the 'fourth pillar of democracy' into another entrepreneurial tool working for the promotion of the commercial interests of the large capitalists. Even countries such as the Soviet Union and India that had very consciously adopted and retained socialism based planned economy for a considerable time, crumbled under the exigencies arising from this drastic transformation. The cardinal rule of profit maximisation around which the capitalist system pivots, transformed media into a tool at the disposal of the crony capitalists. The close alliance between media, business and political forces eroded the democratic ideas and what remained has been a mere delusion of unhindered and unbiased participation by people in the democratic institutions and processes.

Now, the manipulation of electoral outcomes is no more through force and intimidation. It is not done through a rather more sophisticated web of activities that engage and manipulate the electorate at a cognitive level by creating a highly receptive and deceptive narrative woven with the objective of promoting the interests of the highest bidder or strongest owner of this space of communication.

Postscript

The conduct of a majority section of the media that includes both reporters, newsreaders, editors and the management in the recently concluded general election of 2019 in India is another testimony to this blatant construction of a pro-government discourse whereby activists, spoke-persons who did not belong to the NDA and other voices critical of the ruling regime at the regularly held 'Prime-Time' debates also points towards this accentuation of media control intended to reap the desired electoral dividends. Till the time, media would continue to toe-the-line of this alliance of crony capitalism and political elite, it being the fourth pillar of democracy would remain a mere farce. For media to become a true forbearer of individual rights and liberties, it should come out of the shadow of profit generation for its owners and focus on being the people's voice. While newer media avenues have been trying hard to break away from this vicious cycle by generating their own resources through crowd-funding and subscription-based 'free-media', it still is a uphill task. Only then would it reinstate itself into the position of an effective and meaningful player in the electoral area, rather than a pawn of image creation and propaganda machinery.

References and Bibliography

Bahree, Megha (2014), 'Indian Billionaire Gautam Adani Finds a Saviour in the Modi Government', *Forbes* (17-07-2014) [Source: Web] URL: https://www.forbes.com/sites/meghabahree/2014/07/17/adani-finds-a-savior-in-the-modi-govt/#7bbda838639f (Last Accessed on April 28, 2018).

Brijbhushan v *State of Delhi* and *Romesh Thappar* v *State of Madras* (1950).

Business Standard (2016), 'Adani, Ambani had prior knowledge of the Modi government's demonetisation move, says BJP MLA' (27-11-2016) [Source: Web] URL: http://www.business-standard.com/article/current-affairs/adani-ambani-had-prior-knowledge-of-modi-govt-s-demonetisation-move-says-bjp-mla-116111700264_1.html (Last Accessed on April 28, 2018).

Cheony, Anuradha and Rajan Kumar (2017), *Re-emerging Russia: Structures, Institutions and Processes*, Palgrave Macmillan (Digital Edition).

Desai, A.R. (1948), *Social Background of Indian Nationalism,* Popular Book Depot, Bombay.

Gill, Graeme (1998), 'Elites and the Russian Transition', in Graeme Gill (ed.) *Elites and Capitalism*, New York: The New Press.

Goldman, Marshall I. (2003), *The Privatisation of Russia: Russian Reforms Go Awry,* London & New York: Routledge.

Hoffman, David E. (2002), *The Oligarchs: The Embrace of Wealth and Power in New Russia*, New York: Public Affairs Press.

The New Yorker (2019), 'How Journalism Survives: An Interview with Jill Abramson' January 20, 2019, [Source: Web] URL: https://www.newyorker.com/news/the-new-yorker-interview/how-journalism-survives-an-interview-with-jill-abramson (Last Accessed on January 22, 2019).

Kaushik, Krishan (2015), "The Tempest", [Source: web], URL: http://www.caravanmagazine.in/reportage/the-tempest-prannoy-radhika-roy-ndtv (Last Accessed on January 12, 2019).

Khare, Harish (2018) *The Slow Disappearance of Independent Editors from Indian Media*, The Caravan [December 1, 2018] https://caravanmagazine.in/media/slow-disappearance-independent-editors-indian-media.

Kumar, Deepak (2016), *The Trishanku Nation: Memory, Self, and Society in Contemporary India*, Delhi: OUP.

McFaul, Michael (1997), *Russia's Unfinished Revolution: Political Change from Gorbachev to Putin*, Ithaca and London: Cornell University Press.

Nair, Ravi (2017), 'Defence Deals, Crony Capitalism and PM Modi: Did India's 'Nationalist' Government Compromise National Interest?' *Janta ka Reporter* (November 14, 2017) [Source: Web] URL: http://www.jantakareporter.com/india/defence-deals-ambani-adani-modi/159432/ (Last Accessed on April 28, 2018).

Thakurta, Pranjoy Guha et al. (2017), *Modi Governemnt's Rs. 500- Crore Bonanza to the Adani Group*, [Source: Web] URL: https://thewire.in/business/modi-government-adani-group (Last Accessed on April 28, 2018).

The India Freedom Report: Media Freedom and Freedom of Expression in 2017, http://asu.thehoot.org/public/uploads/filemanager/media/THE-INDIA-FREEDOM-REPORT-.pdf (Last Accessed on January 15, 2019).

The Indian Express (2017), 'Biggest Data Leak Reveals Trails of Indian Corporate in Global Secret Tax Havens', November 6, 2017.

Yeltsin, Boris (2000), *Midnight Diaries*, London: Weidenfeld & Nicolson.

Reforms

9

Partial List Based Proportional Representation: A Workable Option in Indian Elections

Jose George

Dr. B.R. Ambedkar's three warnings that he made in his last speech in the Constituent Assembly on adoption of the Indian Constitution on November 25, 1949, *still resonates today*–that political democracy cannot succeed without social and economic democracy. Dr. Ambedkar warned: "On January 26, 1950, we are going to enter into a life of contradictions. In politics we will have equality and in social and economic life we will have inequalities. In politics we will be recognising the principles of one man one vote and one vote one value. In our social and economic life, we shall, by reason of our social and economic structure, continue to deny the principle of one man one vote. How long shall we continue to live this life of contradictions? How long shall we continue to deny equality in our social and economic life? If we continue to deny it for long, we will do so only by putting our political democracy in peril. We must remove this contradiction at the earliest possible moment, or else those who suffer from inequality will blow up the structure of our political democracy."

Even the political democracy and parliamentary system which Ambedkar eulogised in his speech were frequently subject to trial.

The darkest instance was the Indira Gandhi regime's internal emergency period of 1975-77. Current dispensation of Narendra Modi is also witnessing several trials by way of undermining the constitutional institutions and proceeding with presidential system type mannerisms. Even to retain the political democracy guaranteed by the constitution certain institutional mechanisms have to be adopted which may eventually lead to democratisation of the Indian polity and society. A mature electoral system will go a long way in guaranteeing the success of the representative democracy.

Though there are several electoral systems in existence, for the sake of brevity, we can categorise them into three major systems:

(I) the plurality-majority,
(II) the proportional and
(III) the semi-proportional.

(I) Among the plurality-majority group there are three main types that can be identified:

(i) First Past the Post (FPTP)

FPTP is the most popular election system where a candidate gets more votes than all the other candidates, is declared elected, and will be chosen as the representative. This is the electoral system followed in parliamentary democracies in India and the UK.

(ii) Block Vote (BV)

The BV is an electoral system in which a voter can select as many candidates as there are seats. The candidates with the greatest number of votes are elected. If, for example, there are three Council seats up for a particular election, and suppose there are seven candidates for those seats, the top three vote-getters would win the election to those seats. This system is also referred to as plurality-at-large voting or multiple non-transferable voting. This system is followed, in electing members to the Executive Committee of cooperative societies.

(i) The Two-Round System (TRS)

It is not one round election, but takes place in two rounds if required. If no candidate or party receives an absolute majority in the first count, then a second round of voting is held and the winner of this round is declared elected.

(iii) The Alternative Vote (AV)

It is also called instant **runoff.** In this method of election, voters rank candidates in order of preference. If any single candidate receives a majority of first-preference votes, that candidate is declared elected. If no candidate gets 50 per cent plus one votes, the candidate who has the least number of first preference votes is eliminated and that candidate's second preference votes are reapportioned to others and so on till a candidate clears the threshold of 50 per cent of the vote plus one.

(II) The Proportional Representation (PR)

It is another popular system of election prevalent in many countries. PR is recommended to rectify some of the shortcomings in the FPTP. In FPTP the seat is awarded to the individual candidate who receives the most votes in an election from a given constituency. On many occasions a single party or coalition of parties which secured minority votes in legislative bodies may secure majority seats in that legislature. Such a majority will be deciding and implementing their policies even on that majority of people who did not support them during the election. For example, in the 2014 Lok Sabha election the BJP won a majority of 282 seats out of a total of 543 seats with a mere 31 per cent of total votes. No party has ever before won more than half the seats with a vote share of just 31 per cent. The previous lowest vote share for a single-party majority was in 1967, when the Congress won 283 out of 520 seats with 40.8 per cent of the total valid votes polled. In the 2014 Lok Sabha elections the Congress secured 19.3 per cent votes, winning 44 seats, while in 2009, the BJP secured 18.5 per cent votes but won 116 seats. In Uttar Pradesh, the BSP's stronghold, it managed to get 20 per cent of votes, but did not win a single seat. In Tamil Nadu, the DMK and its allies garnered 27 per cent votes and got no seats. In Odisha, the Congress got 26 per cent votes but no seat while the BJP got 22 per cent votes and one seat.

In West Bengal, the Left Front got nearly 30 per cent votes but won only 2 seats. Thirty-one per cent votes were cast for the BJP, which is 20 per cent of the eligible voters, and which is 14 per cent of India's population. That means, potentially, 86 per cent of India, 80 per cent of eligible voters, and 69 per cent of the votes cast were not for the BJP. This means, only 16.5 crores of Indians had voted for the BJP, out of the 54.1 crore people who had bothered to go to the polling booths. Still, the fact of the matter is that the BJP won an absolute majority on its own and it has formed a majority government to govern our country for the 2014 -2019 period. Against this the first-past-the-post–system the proportional Representation (PR) is an electoral system wherein citizens cast their votes for the political parties, and seats are allocated to the parties according to the voting strength they possess.

Among different types of PR system, two important among them are:

(i) The Single Transferable Vote (STV) system as it exists in Ireland. STV uses multi-member districts and voters rank candidates in order of preference on the ballot paper.

(ii) The Proportional Representation–List system: In most cases, this preference marking is optional, and voters are not required to rank-order all candidates; if they wish, they can mark only one. After the total number of first-preference votes is tallied, the count then begins by establishing the quota of votes required for the election of a single candidate. It exists in Israel. The quota used is normally the Droop quota, calculated by the simple formula:

Quota required to win the seat = (total valid votes divided by (number of seats +1)) +1. For instance, suppose the number of valid votes is 100 and the number of seats to be filled are four, then 100 is divided by 4+1 that is 5. The figure we would get is 20. If we add the figure '1' to that we will get the figure '21'. So '21' is the required quota for getting a candidate elected in this case.

The result is determined through a series of counts. At the first count, the total number of first-preference votes for each candidate is ascertained. Any candidate who has the number of first preferences greater than or equal to the quota is immediately declared elected. In the second and subsequent counts, the surplus votes of elected candidates (i.e. those votes above the quota) are redistributed according to the second preferences on the ballot papers. For fairness, the entire candidate's ballot papers can be redistributed, but each at a fractional percentage of one vote, so that the total redistributed votes equal the candidate's surplus (the Republic of Ireland uses a weighted sample instead of distributing fractions). If a candidate had 100 votes, for example, and their surplus was five votes, then each ballot paper would be redistributed according to its second preference at the value of 1/20th of a vote. After any count, if no candidate has a surplus of votes over the quota, the candidate with the lowest total of votes is eliminated. His or her votes are then redistributed in the next count to the candidates left in the race according to the second and then lower preferences shown. The process of successive counts, after each of which surplus votes are redistributed or a candidate is eliminated, continues till either all the seats for the electoral district are filled by candidates who have received the quota, or the number of candidates left in the count is only one more than the number of seats to be filled, in which case all remaining candidates except for one are elected without receiving a full quota.

Party-list proportional representation system and the Proportional Representation–List system as it exists in Israel are a family of voting systems emphasising proportional representation (PR) in elections in which multiple candidates are elected (e.g. elections to parliament) through allocations to an electoral list. They can also be used as part of mixed additional member systems. **List system**, is a method of voting for several electoral candidates, usually members of the same political party, with one mark of the ballot. It is used to elect the parliaments of many West European countries, including Switzerland, Italy and Germany. Electors vote for one of several lists of candidates, usually prepared by the political parties. Each party is granted seats in proportion to the number of popular votes it receives. There are several rules for computing the number of seats awarded to a party, the best known being the "d'Hondt rule" and the "largest-remainder rule." Seats are usually awarded to candidates in the order in which their names appear in the lists. Although ordinarily the list system forces the voters to cast their votes for parties rather than for individual candidates, a number of variations on the system permit voter preferences for individuals to be taken into account.

(III) Partial List Based Proportional Representation or Mixed-Member Proportional (MMP)

It is a mixed electoral system in which voters get two votes: one to decide the representative for their single-seat constituency, and one for a political party. This is a kind of Mixed Electoral system that tends to combine features of the majoritarian, i.e. First Past the Post, Two round systems and the Proportional Representation systems. It is also referred to as Additional Member System (AMS) or Top Up System. Under the MMP system, a set of the seats are allocated using the First Past the Post system whereby the candidates/political parties are voted directly by the electorate in the constituencies and whoever scoops the majority of votes gets the seat. The second set of the seats reallocated using the proportional system to compensate any disproportionality produced by FPTP allocation. For example, a party that gets 10 per cent of the votes nationally, but has got no seat because none of its candidate got a majority will be awarded with 10 per cent of the second set of seats using the PR system. Seats in the legislature are filled firstly by the successful constituency candidates, and secondly, by party candidates based on the percentage of nationwide or region-wide votes that each party received.

MMP was originally used to elect representatives to the German Bundestag. Later, it has been adopted by Bolivia, Lesotho and New Zealand. It was also used in Romania during its 2008 and 2012 legislative elections. In Germany, it is used on the federal level, and in most states. MMP is known as *personalised proportional representation.* In the United Kingdom such systems are used in Scotland, Wales, and the London Assembly, are referred to as additional member systems. In the Canadian province of Quebec, where an MMP model was studied in 2007 is called the *compensatory mixed-member* voting system.

Mixed Member Proportional (MMP) retains the proportionality benefits of Proportional Representation (PR) systems and also ensures that voters have geographical representation. They also have the luxury of two votes, one for the party and one for their local MP. One way is to have one vote for the party list and one vote for your territorial constituency. That is the one way of doing it.

PR systems are a common choice in many new democracies. Over twenty established democracies, and just under half of all 'free' democracies, use some variant of PR. PR systems are dominant in Latin America and Western Europe, and make up a third of all the systems in Africa. While seats are often allocated within regionally-based multi-member districts, in a number of countries (e.g. Germany, Namibia, Israel, Netherlands, Denmark, South Africa, and New Zealand) the parliamentary seat distribution is effectively determined by the overall national vote.

However, in consideration of the level of maturity of the Indian voters and in consideration of voters' expectation to get optimum help from the constituency based representative, a workable suggestion would be the introduction of partial party based list system. If that is introduced, 542 Lok Sabha constituencies in India can be divided into 271 dual member constituencies. Each constituency based voter would be allowed to cast two votes–one for the individual candidate and the second one to the recognised political party at the state/national level. The candidate who gets the maximum votes can be declared as a constituency based representative. The second vote given to the party list can be pooled together and the Election Commission can assign as many party representatives as per the proportion of the vote secured as per the party list published before the election. In order to ensure representation for women, the Election Commission can instruct the political parties to prepare the list of candidates in such a way that every second or third candidate in the list should be a woman. It can have several advantages like reduced influence of *money* and *muscle* power, representation of different linguistic and regional groups in Parliament, etc. The details can be worked out with the help of experts.

The tall claims of the Election Commission, of conducting 'free and fair' elections, ring hollow following the experiences of the 2014 elections. Manipulation of voting machines by hackers to help the BJP to tilt the result in their favour is an open secret now.

With the unabashed and unbridled splurge of money for campaigning, the Election Commission's position has also become questionable. The BJP used its corporate backing to the hilt to launch an advertisement blitzkrieg. The fair practice of allocating equal time to all the national political parties to reach their message to the people of our country through Doordarshan and All India Radio pales in comparison to this. Hundreds of crores of rupees were seized by the Election Commission, but that proved to be only a tip of the iceberg, as thousands of crores more were put into 'buying votes' and went undetected. The BJP was the beneficiary. Naturally the parties that are on the wrong side of the corporates, and stand for the interests of the working class are at a disadvantage in this uneven contest. Money power tilted the balance, setting aside the entire semblance for fairness.

Measures to Strengthen Democracy

Proportional representation helps to contain the influence of money in elections to a large extent. Moreover, as the contest will be directly between parties and not candidates, the influence of caste, religion, region and other parochial considerations too can be reduced. The desired change for a discussion on the policies of the various contesting political parties can be ensured. As people vote for parties, there need not be any worry that their vote will not count. Each vote counts, has an equal value and will add up to decide on the number of seats a political party wins. These are the things that really strengthen a democracy, as all shades of political opinion get a place for representation. Strong opposition, a hallmark of democracy, can check the otherwise possible transformation of parliamentary democracy to fascism. Adolf Hitler became the Chancellor of Germany in 1932 with a mandate of 33.1 per cent of the German electorate. About 66.9 per cent of the Germans did not vote for him, just as 69 per cent of Indians did not vote for Modi.

On Electoral Bonds

The Finance Act, 2017 amended four different statues, namely the Reserve Bank of India Act 1934, The Representation of People's Act 1951, The Income Tax Act 1961 and the Companies Act, 2013 to introduce the concept of Electoral Bonds. The Electoral Bonds was operationalised by the Central Government by issuing a notification on January 2, 2018. What is surprising is that it has been passed by perpetrating a fraud on the constitution by passing it as a money bill, even though it does not qualify as a Money Bill under Article 110 of the Constitution. This is a clear case of manipulation of by-passing the Rajya Sabha since the ruling NDA front did not have majority support in the Rajya Sabha. The electoral bond is a bearer bond in the nature of the promissory note. Selected branches of the State Bank of India are authorised to issue the electoral bonds purchased through a bank account. The system of electoral bonds mostly facilitates corporate funding to the ruling party and opens the way for legitimising bribery and corruption. Companies would be encouraged to provide huge contributions to the ruling party to earn its favour. The electoral bond scheme will make all such kickbacks legal. Now the move to bring about electoral reforms should include the struggle to scrap the electoral bond system and the amendments which have opened up the gates for corporate funding and money coming from foreign sources.

Why India Needs a Proportional Representation System?

A proportional system would give regional parties and independent candidates a better chance of getting into Parliament and bring in different voices to nation-building. The history of South Asia shows that if the leadership is not guided by the spirit of democracy and if the ruling party enjoys an absolute majority in both houses of parliament, then there is every possibility that the ruling clique would soon turn into authoritarian/semi-fascist. India lived through this bitter experience during the 1975-77 internal emergency phase. India is experiencing the repeat of almost the same during the time of Narendra Modi's regime. Unfortunately this is happening in the communally charged atmosphere created by the majority *Hindutva* forces even without declaring a formal emergency and without having a majority in the Rajya Sabha. An electoral system based on complete Proportional Representation, or Partial List based or Mixed Member Proportion (MMD) may not throw up a situation of brute majority. The story of the V.P. Singh government in 1989 and the Deve Gowda ministry in 1996 shows that the absence of brute majority and less opportunity to declare emergency will be useful for the country. After all a coalition ministry with only a simple majority cannot bring more harm to the people. All this justifies the reason for India to opt for a Mixed Member Proportional (MMP) Representation pattern in its legislatures.

Finally, the democratisation of the Indian society in its fullest sense–politically, socially and economically–is the ultimate to guarantee the prevalence of genuine democracy globally in general and in India particularly.

Postscript

In the 17th Lok Sabha election held in 2019, the BJP got 303 seats as per the First Past The Post (FPTP) system, out of a total 542 seats by getting only 37.43 per cent of polled votes. If the figure is converted to proportional representation then they are eligible to get only 202 seats in the Lok Sabha. Since the NDA (National Democratic Alliance) led by the BJP got only 45 per cent votes they are only entitled for 244 seats instead of the actual 353 seats they got now. On the other hand, the Indian National Congress would have got 104 seats in proportion to their 19.51 per cent votes, instead of the actual 52 seats obtained by them now. Instead of their present figure of 91, Congress-led UPA (United Progressive Alliance) would have got 141 seats in proportion to the 26 per cent votes they polled. Partiers and individuals outside NDA and UPA would have got 157 seats in proportion to their total vote share of 29 per cent.

In consideration of the level of maturity of the Indian voters, and in consideration of voters' expectation to get optimum help from the constituency-based representative, in my above given paper, I proposed that a workable suggestion in India would be the introduction of partial party based list system or the Mixed Member Proportional (MMP) Representation system. My proposal was to divide the now existing 542 Lok Sabha constituencies into 271 dual member constituencies. Each constituency based voter would be allowed to cast two votes–one for the individual candidate and the second one to a recognised political party at the state/national level. The candidate who gets maximum votes from the given constituency can be declared as the constituency-based representative. The second vote given to the party list can be pooled together and the Election Commission can assign as many party representatives as per the proportion of the votes secured by each party as per the party list published prior to the election.

In the dual member constituencies for the BJP, it would have been half of 303 that is 152 seats from territorial constituency-wise result and 101 seats from proportional representation since the BJP got only 37.43 per cent of popular votes. It would have made a total of only 252 seats for the BJP out of the 542 seats in the Lok Sabha. The total tally of the BJP-led NDA then would have been 177 from the territorial constituency and 122 from the proportional list system, together making a total of only 299 seats against the present total of 353 seats. In the dual member constituencies for the Congress Party it would have been half of 52 that is 26 seats from territorial constituency-wise result and 53 seats from proportional representation since the Congress got 19.51 per cent of popular votes. It would have made a total of 79 seats for the Congress out of the 542 seats in the Lok Sabha. The total tally of Congress-led UPA then would have been 47 seats from the territorial constituency and

71 seats from the proportional list system, together making a total of 118 seats against the present total of 91 seats.

In a young democracy like India where genuine political, social and economic democracy is still a distant dream, a government with a brute majority would have developed a tendency to turn authoritarian and semi-dictatorial in nature. The dark pages of Indian democracy authored by Indira Gandhi during the 1975-77 internal emergency period can be attributed to the brute majority she got in 1971 (352/518) Lok Sabha election in the aftermath of defeating Pakistan in the December 1970 war and creating Bnagladesh. In the 2019 election Narendra Modi and BJP's narrative was built around communal nationalist jingoism, along with the issues of fighting terrorism after the death of over 40 soldiers in the Pulwama (Kashmir) terror attack on February 14, 2019 and the retaliatory airstrike by the IAF in the Pakistan territory of Balakot soon after. Election campaign by BJP brushed aside all other issues of day-to-day concerns of the people.

History of India shows that if the proportional representation of any type was adopted in Indian elections, no government would have come to power with a brute majority. A government not having brute majority will have no option but to run the government through a consensus of different party representatives in the Parliament. At least their capability to do harm to the people would be limited.

So in the light of the 2019 and earlier Lok Sabha elections, the author is of the opinion that a system of proportional representation would have been better for the health of Indian democracy. The history of countries like Israel and Germany shows that absence of absolute majority for a single party would not affect the vigour and progress of a country. All this definitely justifies author's stand for introducing the proportional system of representation in the Indian elections.

10

Electronic Voting: A Leap Forward in Election Reforms

Rohidas Mundhe

The low turnout during the election is one of the concerned areas not only for the Election Commission, different associations and Indian government but also to the Western countries as well where participation in the voting process is low. The voters, so-called intellectuals, academicians, policy makers, traders, educated youths and so forth to whom we listen, watch and read in newspapers, books, on TV and in public gatherings remain out of the voting process. Once this class starts taking part in all the elections from Gram Panchayat to Parliamentary election, the candidates without vision for their wards, village, constituency, district, state and nation as a whole will not be elected or they will be discouraged. The candidates with a criminal background and political background without calibre and vision will remain out of the law-making process. Only the sincere and committed candidates will get elected. Money and muscle power will have no place in politics if technology such as giving voting rights on internet and mobiles is used to increase the participation of the voters.

India has had sixteen general elections to the Lok Sabha so far. Over the period of time, the number of eligible voters went up from

17.3 crores in 1951 to 83.40 crores in 2014. While the number of registered voters has increased continuously from the first general election in 1951 to sixteenth general in 2014, but the voter turnout has been mixed. At the same time 53 political parties contested the election in 1951, whereas 465 political parties contested in 2014. There is a 9 fold increase in political parties contesting elections but voting turnout remained mostly between 55 to 60 per cent. To increase the voting percentage, the 2014 general election in India seems historic in many ways. It was the first general election in the history of Indian politics where technology was used tremendously, ranging from Facebook, Email, SMSs and twitter to 3D technology. But the moot questions like whether such efforts really helped to increase the participation of voters? Why is there low participation of the voters? In this context, it is necessary to understand the following factors.

- The behaviour pattern of the young and old voters.
- Examination of the election reforms that are made to increase the voting percentage.
- The use of technology and its effect on voters and their response to it.
- The role of political parties in educating the voters to take part in the voting process.
- What kind of reforms the voters are expecting so that they will cast their votes in all elections.

The efforts are continuously being made by political parties, Election Commission, different institutions and associations to increase the participation of voters, but the response is not up to expectation. In the 2014 general election, different agencies and associations came up with new ideas such as Indian Medical Association declared during 2014 general election that those voters who cast their votes would get 25 per cent concession in doctors' fees in Gadchiroli district of Maharashtra. In Delhi, the Federation of All India Petroleum Traders also declared Rs. 0.50 concession in petrol per litre to those who have cast their votes on Election Day. To motivate and encourage the voters, particularly the young voters, the Election Commission through its Youth Team initiative tried to motivate the college students to participate in the voting process. Not only this but the Election Commission went ahead to ensure that no eligible person remained outside the voting process. In the 2014 general election, all arrangements were made by the Election Commission to ensure that Darshandas, a temple priest, got to cast his vote. The Commission had set up a booth only for him in the Una Assembly constituency. If the booth was not set up he would have to travel 20 kms to cast his vote.

When we take into account the efforts made by the Election Commission and the aftermath of election, these efforts seem either fallen short or people did not like this because, if we see the data from the 1st general election to the 16th general election, the average voting is 60 per cent. That also varies from state to state and region to region within the state. Only in the year 1984 after the assassination of Indira Gandhi and in 2014 the voting percentage was 64 and 66 respectively. The lowest turnout was in the 14th general election in 2004, 58.7 per cent. It seems that the appeal from different associations and agencies is not transforming into action for big Indian cities when it comes to participating in large numbers to vote for their favourite candidates in polls. Despite a high urban base with a more discerning and affluent electorate, witnessing a low turnout in elections, local or general, is the adage for these cities. Notwithstanding the huge cry made through promotional activities and advertisements, cities like Mumbai, Delhi, Bangalore, Hyderabad, Chennai and Ahmedabad hardly believe in exercising their franchise to elect the 'right' candidates in the municipal corporations' polls, as shown by the low voting percentage each time. It needs to understand that, is it because of the behaviour of politicians who talk big but do not make a difference once they are in power? There is a sizeable discrepancy between the willingness of young people to vote compared with their middle-aged and elderly counterparts. Actually, it has always been true that young and highly educated people are less likely to vote than the rest of the population, but the gap between different age groups has grown over time.

It is said and widely discussed in media, parliament, and various academic and non-academic forums that due to non-worthy candidates contesting elections, voters are not casting their votes. For this, anti-corruption crusader Anna Hazare demanded None of The Above option. He also urged the voters to use the "none of the above" (NOTA) if they find no candidate is suitable to represent them. The Election Commission also introduced this option but very few people actually used it. This sort of initiative or election reform could not help to increase the voting turnout. But it does not mean that the people do not wish to vote during the election period. There are other reasons/obstacles for not exercising the franchise. There are many voters who are away from their voting stations. For example, migrant workers from one state to another state, from one city to another city within the state and from village to city are unwilling/unable to cast their vote on the Election Day due to inconvenience. Similarly, there are many students studying in different cities and states within the country who are away from the polling places. Moreover, as the data revealed by the Ministry of External Affairs in 2017 shows that there are 7,52,725 Indian students who are studying abroad. The US continues to be the preferred destination for Indians pursuing higher education abroad, with Canada and Australia taking the second and third spots. There are employed people in unorganised, government and private sectors in India as well as abroad. There are merchants, industrialists, tourists, who are away, either in India or abroad, from their voting places on the voting day. If we calculate this number, certainly it is in millions. All these are educated voters but owing to certain compulsions or difficulties they are unable to cast their votes.

To bring them into the voting process, it is necessary to use existing technology as well as explore new technology to overcome such difficulties. One such technology is the "internet" and "mobile phone" to be used for voting purposes. We use this technology on a daily basis for booking tickets, transferring money, sending text messages but why we are not using the same technology for electing our representatives who make laws for us? Very advanced technology is used in the field of space science, earth observation, GPRS to navigate the aircraft and so forth but the same/simple technology is not used for voting purposes. If internet and mobile phones are used for voting purposes, this will certainly increase the voting percentage, at least by 20 to 25 per cent from the present average of 60 per cent to 80 to 85 per cent. The people living in any part of the country and abroad can use this method to cast their votes and elect the right candidate. When educated people start taking part in the election process, no political party will dare to sponsor the candidates who are unconcerned regarding their village, wards, constituencies, districts, state and nation as a whole. Those candidates have a criminal record and corrupt background. Political parties will also take note of these new voters and their aspirations while giving tickets to such candidates. This will lead to more competitive and qualitative politics and will reduce the politics of muscles and money.

There is a possibility to raise the question about the safety and secrecy of such a voting method. Because, questions have been raised regarding the existing electronic voting machine but no political party has proved that the electronic voting machine can be tampered. Even then, the Election Commission has used Voter Verifiable Paper Audit Trial Machines (VVPATM) in the recent assembly election in Madhya Pradesh in 2018 to maintain and prove the authenticity of the EVMs. Similarly, if we find any error or misuse of the mobile and internet voting, the Election Commission and government will take necessary steps to correct it.

However, to opt for the old method like ballot paper, is not a solution because there are incidents of booths capturing and bogus voting. In the recent parliamentary election held in December 2018, in Bangladesh, the Awami League Party led by Sheikh Hasina won 287 seats out of 298 seats. However, the opposition parties said the results were farcical because of claims of vote-rigging and called for fresh elections. The Bangladesh media and people around the world also raised questions and expressed the will to inquire into the matter. The United States expressed concern over reports of irregularities during the Bangladesh elections and said it "undermined faith in the electoral process". The UN spokesperson, Secretary-General Antonio Guterres said, "The United Nations is aware of violent incidents and reports of irregularities in the Bangladesh general election." Bangladesh uses the ballot paper system. Do we want to opt for such old methods where there is no guarantee of free, fair, cost effective and errorless election? So, the technological error should be tackled with the upgradation of technology.

We have seen the misuse of ATM cards or credit cards like transferring of money from somebody's account to another account or withdrawing money, which is also called cyber-crime, but does it mean that either government or RBI is going to stop using the ATM and credit cards? The banks have come up with the solution to this problem by using chip in the cards. Earlier they used ATM or credit cards with black strip to cover the secret code number. If there is a misuse of electronic voting we will see how it has been used and accordingly it can be dealt with technologically. This new method of voting should start on an experimental basis from any small state like Goa or any other state from the North East region to understand how it works and how voters respond to this. This will reduce the burden on the security personnel during elections and reduction in expenditure. Similarly, those people who are constantly under the threat of missing the casting of vote can use this technology sitting at home without fear and favour.

Postscript

The 17th general election to the Lok Sabha was over on May 19, 2019 with the last voting phase. As many as 669 parties contested the election this time compared to 465 political parties in the 2014 general election. This is the first Lok Sabha election in which all EVMs were backed by VVPAT machines. The Election Commission made a concerted effort to conduct free and fair elections. Even in the unbearable temperature, in all the seven phases voters enthusiastically participated in the election process. The total turnout stood at 67.36%, the highest turnout in a Lok Sabha election, 1% more than in 2014. Some of the states experienced a very high turnout such as Andhra 80.5% than Telangana 62.8%. Turnout was particularly high in Jharkhand 84%, West Bengal 82% and Madhya Pradesh 77%. Maharashtra recorded 62% turnout while Delhi and Uttar Pradesh 60%. Jammu and Kashmir recorded the lowest turnout. There was controversy over the use of EVMs and possible misuse of the EVMs. Therefore, almost twenty-one political parties met the Election Commission and requested for counting of all the VVPAT slips and match them with the EVMs number. But at the eleventh hour the Election Commission was not prepared due to lack of human resources and certain rules need to be changed to count all the slips. Physical verification of VVPAT slips with the EVM count was done across over 20,000 polling stations on May 23 before declaration of results as per the Supreme Court orders. In a verdict delivered by the Supreme Court on PIL filed regarding the 100% count of the VVPAT slips, the Court refused to count all the slips but it was keener on the logistics of physical verification in its April 8 judgment. It said the VVPAT verification of five EVMs, rather than 125 polling booths, was far more "viable at this point of time" in the Lok Sabha poll season. It had added that verification of five EVMs would not be a drain on the ECI's infrastructural resources and manpower. After the declaration of the results on May 23, 2019, no political party raised any doubt about the EVMs either with the Election Commission or Supreme Court. For the first time, women closed the gap to male voters. The recent trend in Indian politics has witnessed that people are choosing single party government whether it is in State Assemblies or Lok Sabha, i.e. Arunachal Pradesh, Odisha, Sikkim and the Central Government.

References

Achin Vanaik and K.C. Suri (2013), *Political Science*, Vol. 2, Oxford University Press.

Dushyantha Mendis (2008), *Electoral Process and Governance in South Asia*, Sage Publications, New Delhi.

G.S. Gill (2008), 'Election Result Forecasting Using Two Layer Perception Network', *Journal of Theoretical and Applied Information Technology*, 4 (11), 1019.

IANS (2019), US expresses concern over violence, irregularities in Bangladesh polls, https://www.business-standard.com/article/international/us-expresses-concern-over-violence-irregularities-in-bangladesh-polls-119010200017_1.html, January 2, 2019.

India Today (2018), Low voter turnout, uncontested wins in J&K civic polls: Srinagar to create history with BJP mayor?, https://www.indiatoday.in/india/jammu-and-kashmir/story/low-voter-turnout-uncontested-wins-in-j-k-civic-polls-srinagar-to-create-history-with-bjp-mayor-1369041-2018-10-16, October 16, 2018.

Indian Express (2018), Jammu and Kashmir Urban Local Bodies polls: Only 4.2 per cent voter turnout in final phase, http://www.newindianexpress.com/nation/2018/oct/16/jammu-and-kashmir-urban-local-bodies-polls-only-42-per-cent-voter-turnout-in-final-phase-1886302.html, October 16, 2018.

J. Eldersved (1951), 'Theory and Method in Voting Behaviour' Research, *Journal of Politics*, 13 (1), 70-87.

Myron Weiner and John Osgood Field (eds.) (1983), *Electoral Politics in the Indian State*, 5 Vols., Manohar Publications, New Delhi.

Paul Wallance and Ramashray Roy (2003), *India's 1999 Election and 20th Century Politics*, Sage Publications, New Delhi.

Peter Ronald Desouza and E. Sridharan (2006), *Indian Political Parties*, Sage Publications, New Delhi.

Ramashray Roy and Paul Wallace (2007), *India's 2004 Election: Grass Root and National Perspectives*, Sage Publications, New Delhi.

Rasheeduddin Khan (1969), *Political Participation and Political Change in Andhra Pradesh*, Osmania University, Hydrabad.

S. Kumar (2009), Delhi Assembly Election, *EPW*, 44 (6), 27-30.

S. Shastri, K.C. Suri and Yogendra Yadav (2009), *Electoral Politics in Indian States: Lok Sabha Election in 2004 and Beyond*, Oxford University Press, New Delhi.

Sanjay Kumar and Praveen Rai (2013), *Measuring Voting Behaviour in India*, Sage Publications, New Delhi.

Suhas Palshikar and Yogendra Yadav (2014), *Party Competition in Indian State*, Oxford University Press, New Delhi.

The Avenue Mail (2014), India's democracy reaches out to lone voter in Gir forest https://www.avenuemail.in/india/indias-democracy-reaches-lone-voter-gir-forest/39453/, April 20, 2014.

The Daily Star (2019), UN Calls for Restraints, https://www.thedailystar.net/bangladesh-national-election-2018/united-nations-urges-maintain-post-elections-peace-in-bangladesh-1681474, January 2, 2019.

The Hindu (2018), US continues to be preferred destination for Indian students; UAE sees a surge https://www.thehindu.com/education/us-continues-to-be-preferred-destination-for-indian-studentsuae-sees-a-surge/article24533290.ece, July 27, 2018.

Contributors

Ali, Zaheer (Prof.), academic, activist and writer. Chairman of Centre for Promotion of Democracy and Secularism, zaheeali@gmail.com

George, Jose (Dr.), formerly Professor and Head, Department of Civics and Politics, University of Mumbai, josegeorgem@gmail.com

Jain, Ranu (Dr.), Professor, Centre for Studies in Sociology of Education, Tata Institute of Social Sciences, Mumbai, ranutapi@gmail.com

Jal, Murzban (Dr.), Director, Centre for Educational Studies, Indian Institute of Education, Pune and a prolific writer, murzbanjal@hotmail.com

Momin, Noorjahan (Dr.), Assistant Professor, Faculty of Law, Jamia Millia Islamia, New Delhi, mnoorjahan@jmi.ac.in

Mundhe, Rohidas (Dr.), Assistant Professor, Department of Civics and Politics, University of Mumbai, mundejnu@gmail.com

Shakir, Shuja (Dr.), Associate Professor in Political Science, Dr. Babasaheb Ambedkar Marathwada University, Aurangabad, shujashakir@rediffmail.com

Srinivasulu, K. (Dr.), Senior Fellow, ICSSR, Professor (Retd.), Department of Political Science, Osmania University, Hyderabad, srinivasulukarli@gmail.com

Wankhede, Harish (Dr.), Assistant Professor, Centre for Political Studies, Jawaharlal Nehru University, New Delhi, enarish@gmail.com

Yadav, Rasu Chhatrapati, Assistant Professor, Department of Journalism, Osmania University, Hyderabad, pursuing PhD Programme in Journalism, chatrapatiy@gmail.com